Twelve Miles
From the Rest of the World

A Portrait of the Damariscotta River

Barnaby Porter   Al Trescot

Twelve Miles From the Rest of the World
A Portrait of the Damariscotta River

Photography copyright © 2005 Al Trescot
Text copyright © 2005 Barnaby Porter
Book Creation copyright © 2005 Al Trescot

Library of Congress Catalog Card Number 2005902230
ISBN 0-9767321-0-6

Limited edition prints of the photographs in this book may be obtained from Rocky Hill Publishing.

A Crow Point & Rocky Hill Design publication
Damariscotta River, Maine ◊ 2005

Rocky Hill Publishing • 13 Lilac Garden Lane • Damariscotta, Maine 04543
207-563-5539 • www.rockyhillpublishing.com
Printed in U.S.A. by J.S. McCarthy, Augusta, Maine

Introduction

Al and I have frequently joked about how this book was first conceived. "Basically," he said to me one day, "it all started with just a couple of guys out messing around in a boat." I guess I'd have to say he got it about right. But it was a little more involved than that … and the Damariscotta River ought to figure in there somewhere.

We first got to know each other a few years ago. I am a woodworker with artistic ambitions who needed his graphic design skills on a couple of projects. We became friends. I then launched a new boat, named *Old Crow*, in September 2003. Al, at the same time, had just purchased a very fancy new camera and had shown an interest in my boat, so I invited him out for a cruise on the Damariscotta.

As we made our way downriver, he began clicking away, and I would say something like, "If you think those rocks were nice, wait'll you see what I've got to show you." And we would go on that way, and I would tell him a story, or an incident that had happened at such and such a spot. We were having a great time, and Al came with me frequently after that.

One afternoon, it finally dawned on us that we had pretty much canvassed the entire river, when Al said something about how many people around here have never really seen this, and then, "Hey! We ought to do a book." I couldn't have agreed more.

This book has been on my mind for a long time. I have wanted to write it not only for my own satisfaction in celebrating this river I know as home, but to share it with those who have somehow missed it for whatever reason.

It is the sense of place that I have tried to communicate, and the manner of seeing it I've found so rewarding. Each individual will see something different; that doesn't matter; it's supposed to be personal.

The book might never have been made had it not been for my fortuitous collaboration with Al Trescot. Not only did he do all of the photography, he created the book. Al is responsible for virtually every detail of the publication you hold in your hands – the cover design, the font style, the total layout, even the paper it's printed on.

Having said that, his greatest contribution to this project has been his enthusiasm and companionship, and I should add that of all the people I have taken out on the river, Al has been the sharpest eyed and keenest observer ever. Out the thousands of photographs he took, there is not a single one he cannot pinpoint as to its location, date and time of day. I think it would be fair to say that he has inhaled the Damariscotta River in all its moods and seasons and savored every minute of it. I could not have had a more ideal partner in this endeavor.

This is a very personal portrait of a river. Every portrait of a subject will be different from all others of course, and because two hands have worked this one on the same canvas, the difference between the left and the right might be apparent from time to time. Al has captured the subject with his camera. I have attempted to paint it with words.

Barnaby Porter
Damariscotta River, 2005

Prentiss Cove looking toward the river

The First Good Look

The first good look at this river, the one I've lived and worked on pushing forty years, rests fixed in my memory. It was a clear, cool morning in early April. There were patches of snow still in the pine woods here on the Walpole shore. A hermit thrush was singing, and a woodpecker's loud hammering echoed through the tall trees.

I was fresh out of the University of Maine and unemployed. My wife, Susan, and I were that day starting the job of opening up the dense understory of firs in the woodlot where my parents planned to build a house. The firs weren't very big, six to ten feet, but they were thick, and there were four acres of them. Not owning a chainsaw, we went at the task with an ax, a pair of clippers, and, what turned out to be the best tool, an exceedingly sharp machete.

Our routine was to chop and hack and clip fir trees and pile brush until noon. Then we'd take lunch on the shore. After lunch we'd work as late as we could stand it, or until Susan threatened mutiny, whichever came first.

That first morning was really the beginning of our love affair with the Damariscotta River. All the elements were in those April woods by the shore – the breathless, cool air under the huge pines; the smell of balsam and salt water; nuthatches and chickadees flitting about, their calls mingling with those of the thrushes and the cries of gulls; here and there the forest floor decorated with a clam shell or mussel dropped by a crow among the pincushion mosses; an occasional boat passing by on the river; and … that vast, silver expanse of water out there.

Much the way I have seen so many others do over the years, we stood on the shore that day and tried to imagine the rest of the river beyond where it bent out of sight, upriver and down, commenting that it appeared more like a long lake than the river we knew it to be. Never could we have guessed at that moment how intimate our relationship with this place would become. Then, as we sat munching tuna fish sandwiches, we suddenly became aware of a deer's head trailing a wake on the water, coming in our direction. When the deer reached the shore very near where we were, it clambered up onto the rocks, shook and bounded quickly up into the woods. That was the beginning.

In the decades since, we have lived in East Boothbay; east Edgecomb, in the vicinity of Merry Island; Damariscotta; and now, here to stay, in Walpole, on Crow Point, by the little island at the mouth of Prentiss Cove — all this time, on or near the river. It has been the constant thread and an ever-present influence in our lives, particularly mine, as it has related to my work history, one way or another, through the years.

The river has not only been a prominent source of our daily exaltations over its beauty and natural wonders, but it has also added a far-ranging dimension to our world and routines, from recreation to daily meditation, from food-gathering to storm-watching, and from simply messing around on it in boats to dreaming of where it could some day take us from here. The Damariscotta is twelve miles of heaven … a natural treasure in our midst. And it's home.

The Grand Tour

It takes anywhere from four to six hours at my usual pace, which is leisurely and conversational. That's too slow for most of the kids I know, at least those who have endured it once or twice before. They'd rather ride with my friend, "Wild Bill," who tears up and down the middle of the river at thirty plus miles an hour, the shortest distance and time between points A and B being first and foremost in all their minds. The way I see it, such flying passages miss a lot.

Many years ago on a foggy afternoon, I had Bill and his sister captive in my old boat, and I took them on an abbreviated version of my river tour just to show them a few of my favorite spots. They both were very appreciative; I figured I had managed to open these relative newcomers' eyes to some of the more exquisite, out-of-the-way delights of the Damariscotta. My pleasure.

Not long after that, though, Bill coined a new term for what I do when I'm out on the river: "Coving" — as in, "Hey, y'all want to come along with me … or go coving with Barnaby?" I liked the expression. It pretty well describes what I do, which is stay close to shore and meander in and out of every cove and hideaway that the height of tide will allow.

Damariscotta

7 k

A full tour would begin at the town landing in Damariscotta at the head of the river, preferably with a packed lunch and a couple of fishing rods. At the start, it might be worth discussing the origins of the unusual name, "Damariscotta." It is after all the name of this river as well as the town, so something should be said. The only sure fact is that no one knows the whole truth of the matter. And, according to my atlas, it is the only Damariscotta in the world.

The most charming explanation is that it comes from the Abenaki word, "tamescot," for "alewife place," acknowledging the historic abundance of these fish on their migratory runs through to the head of the river. Indeed, an early (1666) map of this region had labeled our river, "taniscot" – pretty close. I'd be quite willing to accept this as the whole story, except for the mighty curious similarity between the names "Damariscotta" and "Damariscove" Island off the river's mouth. Though spelled many different ways in the years closely following the island's first settlement as a fishing camp, the early histories seem to suggest it was first laid claim to by a Humphrey Damarill. And because of that island's key role in the settlement of this immediate region, it doesn't exercise my imagination too much to simply conclude that Humphrey's last name got hybridized with the Abenaki's beloved "Tamescot," spelled any way folks back then could dream up.

One thing clear is that the twin villages of Damariscotta and Newcastle have strong historical connections to the river, as it, like most rivers, was the main highway in the very early years, allowing access to its bordering land, the resources therein, the relatively easy shipment of

Lingering Sunset

Leaden grey overhead, wispy pink on its western edge, the end-of-day, mid-March sky holds no promise of warmth this evening as the setting sun stabs its cold, golden beams through one last snow squall driving across the river.

Just a reminder, lest I forget in my longing for the next season, that there is no denying our astronomical circumstances and the calendar. And to underscore this, the light darkens to lavender, sky and water, wavelets stiffing in the breeze, and the afternoon's dusting of snow lends its thin whiteness to the settling twilight hour.

It is my habit, indeed the human habit, to gaze appreciatively on that setting sun. We are sun watchers after all. And, no matter how spectacular the light and the clouds, no matter how breathtaking the show, there is always the sense that day is losing to night, light to darkness, warmth to cold, familiarity to the unknown.

Once the sun goes down, it's gone – a death – and so I watch until there is no more.

A winter sunset from the parking lot, Damariscotta

goods and normal travel. An aerial photograph of Damariscotta, even today after various landfill projects, shows it to be more *in* the river than alongside it. I sincerely wish I could have seen the days when there were numerous shipyards and wharfs in both towns, some of them right up against the back of the buildings on Main Street; the days when newly launched ships well over 200 feet in length would have sailed right past my house, destined for places like China and San Francisco; the days when steam boats made regular, daily runs up and down the river highway. The last four-masted schooner was launched in 1922.

I can only imagine how those busy times might have compared with the relative serenity of today, and how different the surrounding valley must have seemed with most of its forests cut down for fuel and lumber and to clear the land for farming. Aside from the obvious industries of fishing and shellfish harvesting directly from the river itself, and the above mentioned shipbuilding and farming, there were brickyards, sawmills, ice houses, saltworks, ferry landings and, here and there where the geography was favorable, clusters of houses and support buildings and maybe a store – all centers of activity for the populace who lived hard by the river up and down both shores.

Although I am no historian, as I cruise its waters, I cannot help trying to imagine what it must have been like then, and even before then, when the ice ages first formed and gave birth to the Damariscotta River I now recognize as home.

The location of the "Reversing Falls" in the upper river between the bridge and Great Salt Bay..

Oyster Creek looking toward Great Salt Bay

Pushing off, we head downriver, threading through the motley collection of pleasure and fishing boats moored in front of Schooner Landing restaurant and Barroll's Point (called Jacks Point on the chart) on the Newcastle side. Lewis Barroll, who owned the big yellow house and barn on that point with its beautiful grounds, was, one day back in 1955, the unprepared host to a scene of theatrical romance right out of the movies, literally. He called his daughter, Penny Walker (who lives in that house today) to tell her that her heart-throb, Gordon MacRae, and his co-star, Shirley Jones, were right that minute out in the barn having their hair done and their makeup put on. The yard was full of trucks and cars, cameras and huge lights and about fifty people, movie directors and technicians.

They had come to shoot that (now) famous scene in the film musical, *Carousel,* in which Bill and Julie sing "If I Loved You" under a big maple tree with a white bench around it. That maple tree still stands there today.

The Little City … smelt shacks on Great Salt Bay

13

"Pukka", a Riverside 24, built by Paul Bryant from a design by Paul's father, Creston. "Pukka" is hull #18.

A Tug on My Line

With the coming of peas and lettuce in the garden, lilacs and lupine, hawkweed and sow-thistle and swaying timothy and orchard grass and, yes, mosquitoes, June settles over the land like a lush, green wave in all its many hues. The oaks and maples fill out with full, dark leaves, while the hemlocks and firs, in layered boughs, primp themselves with the pale, green tips of new branchlets. Such is June, bursting in all its vitality.

I see it out in the river too, where rafts of young eiders, whole flotillas, ply their way among the ledges. Under their busy, little webbed feet, mussels let out silky jets of spawn, and, overhead, an osprey labors in the direction of the island, repeatedly, with stick after stick to mend and build up even further its bristling nest.

And of course it's June, too, when the jellyfish again fill the green water like so many pale, white, pulsing parachutes, telling me it's time to trail a line behind the boat for mackerel. I know they're there, that I'll catch one, but oh how I long for the surprise of that first and sudden pull on the line.

When at last one does grab my hook, there again is that old, familiar tug, immediately recognizable, like a knock on the door of a long-time friend, who will soon appear in iridescent green alongside.

Then, rounding the first red nun past Barroll's Point, there, off to the right on the Newcastle shore again, rests a pleasing confusion of low, grey and white buildings, cradled boats, a tall gin pole, vintage trucks and an old tractor at the head of a hauling ramp leading down to the water. This is Riverside Boat Company, a boat yard that has been in the Bryant family for over two hundred years. The first Bryants migrated here from Cape Cod around 1790 and began building boats in Damariscotta Mills. Today, in its present location, where the Bryants had once operated a brickyard, the boat company is run by Paul Bryant and his son, Nathaniel, and still specializes in the construction of fine wooden boats, complete restorations and repairs – a healthy and thriving remnant of the past. As many along the Damariscotta feel, Paul's relationship with the river and how it relates to his life's work are paramount. He will never leave this place; neither will Nathaniel.

The next two and a half miles of the "upper river" hold true to what that characterization suggests. Low water depths barely exceed twenty feet in the meandering channel, if that, and on drain tides, great areas of mudflats are exposed. The town outskirts, represented by closely spaced houses very near the shore, extend down a way about as far as Hog Island and Huston Cove on the east side. Looking back over our wake at this point, the twin villages of Damariscotta and Newcastle, joined by the bridge and bookended by the church steeples at either end, spread out in the most pleasing panorama.

Sunset on a frozen river, Schooner Landing's pier at right

Not a Night to be Out

The river froze the night before as it started to snow. It was a day for holing up. Damariscotta's Main Street was the way I prefer it: filled with snow, storm-lovers shuffling about, unlimited parking space for those with the right tires, and with the peaceful atmosphere of a town resigned to the unavoidable truth of a slow business day. The wind blew hard, forty miles an hour, and the snow continued and never let up, even as darkness fell. With the storm apparently gathering itself for a second full night, the countryside braced for whatever was to come.

It certainly was not a night for casual outings. Ten to fifteen minutes simply to warm a vehicle and to clear the frost from both inside and outside the windshield. Three or four degrees was all it was, not brutal, but, combining with the storm, not a night to be out. No one needed an excuse to hunker down and stay put by the fire. On the waterfront, Schooner Landing Restaurant and Bar huddled on it's forest of pilings held fast in the ice, the place locked up, closed

this night, the swirls of snow whipping around its rooftops, unseen and unthought-of as they trailed downriver into the darkness, the place locked up, closed this night. Inside, a dim amber light fed quietly in the emptiness.

It was a fire worthy of that howling winter night, a night no one had planned to be out and about. By the time I got there, the parking lot by the town landing was full of cars and pickup trucks with their motors running. They were full of people scratching at the frost on their windows. An unabashed gawker, I weaved my way to the front ranks.

There in the night blizzard stood the burning building, a terrible and beautiful sight, the unexpected details of which made sense when I saw them. The spotlights from six towns' worth of fire trucks played on the scene. Huge, billowing, orange flames leaped upward through the curtains of heavy, horizontally blowing snow, and hissing jets of water from the fire hoses shot in great arcs, up and over and into the night.

Windows popped, ceilings fell, and the letters, "Schooner Landing," on the gable end toward us were gradually seared and scorched by the heat and licking flames until at last they spelled "Defeated," or so it seemed. The whole raging scene was lit in a giant dome of firelight against the flying snow.

I sat and watched for an hour … and more. It saddened me to see the fireball billowing into the same dining room where I had enjoyed so many meals with friends, to see the heavy smoke spewing from the same kitchen where my son had worked at his first summer job, washing dishes, to see this prime piece of real estate at the head of the river as it was utterly consumed with the violent abandon of such a fire.

I thought some, too, of the effect on the unseen. What of the millions of tiny lives that lingered down under, under the wharf, under the ice below — the barnacles on pilings, the mussels, and on the littered mud bottom, the myriad worms and mud shrimp, the hermit crabs? How would this change things for them? Would the noxious poisons from this conflagration reach into their world?

Just then, a pigeon, like the proverbial bat out of Hell, flapped in terrified confusion out from its roost under the wharf. Then another and another. Smoke, flames, streaming jets of water, spinning red lights, spotlights, headlights, grumbling trucks, shouting men, blasting snow and wind and only four degrees of temperature. Theirs was a desperate plight.

And the men working at this blaze, who would otherwise have been drowsing at home this night — they were having their difficulties too. A drenched pair of firefighters struggled with a hose's coupling. Ice was forming on everything around them, including themselves, and they were freezing right to their bones. When they were momentarily interrupted by coffee-bearing women from the café across the street, the story goes, they shouted, "Good God, yes, throw it on us!"

It was not a good night to be out, but it happened that way. The next morning was bright and clear. The storm had passed. The building on the wharf, what was left, sagged under the weight of tons of cindered gray ice, the charred remains a carbon copy of that stormy night. And down below, the forest of oak pilings was multiplied by an infinity of icicles.

It is along this stretch that one begins to see much evidence of the river's burgeoning oyster industry, another thriving remnant of the far past – long floating strings of meshed grow-out trays, bowing gracefully in the current, often populated by resting and preening sea birds, and floating work platforms with washing and sorting gear, stacked high with more trays. Although the next several miles will bear witness, here and there, to aquaculture and the Damariscotta's superior oyster growing environment, it is this upper river that I think of as "Oyster Alley."

The question arises in my mind: Where did most of the oysters grow that resulted in the early Indians' truly remarkable (and much wondered about) shell heaps above the bridge in town? Worldwide, there are very few such middens to rival them. And I find myself talking with my friend, and long-time oyster grower, Gil Jaeger, who has pondered the same thing. The consensus seems to be that most of the oysters must have grown in the upper river, as transporting such huge quantities as represented by the middens doesn't make much sense. And the vast extent of the shell heaps strongly suggests they were much more likely the result of a food production operation (shucking and smoking perhaps), laying up stores for the long winters, than simply the remnants of a long string of Saturday night suppers tossed out the doors of so many wigwams.

Coupled with this is a further notion posited by some that the large Salt Bay above the heaps could, at one time, have harbored far more favorable conditions for oysters than is the case today. Past changes in sea level, water circulation, salinity, sedimentation and even more recent human activities (Sawmills? Shipyards?) and alterations, could well have obscured the prehistoric condition from our curious scrutiny. It could be that Salt Bay sustained very heavy oyster populations in the distant past.

From the break in the river at the green day-beacon below Hog Island, things open up and one gets the first longshot view downriver, where, with any respectable southerly breeze, the chop can pick up a bit. It is here, too, where the scenery takes on a more pastoral aspect – some older houses on the high ground, meadows leading down to the shore. Close inspection, here and there, reveals the remnants of an old, stone wharf and brickyard, paths down to the water to seldom used landing spots and places that suggest they've seen more vigorous activity in bygone years. There are several rock formations on the west side in the vicinity of that day-beacon that are particularly pretty, as well as a spectacular example of such a mile or so further down on the east side that is pictured on the cover of a book I know. With its gnarled old pines and wandering roots clinging to the wavy ledges, it looks much like a Japanese bonsai garden.

Mussels and Science

Back in the early years of commercial aquaculture in Maine, nearly thirty years ago, I was a participant in the first fledgling enterprise to acquire a license and lease area in the state, and it was right here on the Damariscotta River. Pioneered by Ed Myers at Abandoned Farm in Clarks Cove, the operation concerned itself primarily with the cultivation of blue mussels, one of the fastest growing, most efficient feeding and highest-in-protein shellfish in the world.

While already here in vast natural abundance, it is well known that mussels suspended in the water column for their whole lives, rather than growing intertidally (out of water for several hours of every tidal cycle), produce a much higher quality product by virtue of the fact they are feeding continuously and growing faster. The shells are much thinner and lighter; the meat is younger and more tender; disease and parasite problems are diminished along with the potential for tooth-breaking pearls.

I was hired as biological and technical consultant, which dovetailed very nicely with work I had been doing next door at the Darling Marine Center. While occupied thus, I learned some very interesting things about the river, not the least of which was that it turned out to be a perfect natural laboratory.

One of my experiments involved twelve experimental mussel rafts (XMRs), moored one every mile the length of the river (#1 in South Bristol - #12 above the bridge in Newcastle), in March through November, for five years. I designed them to enable me to measure the monthly growth and mortality rates of captive, known-age seed mussels at each station, and to measure the rate of natural spatfall (mussel "fouling") at each location as well. In addition, I measured water temperature and salinity monthly.

Without laboring through the data, what emerged from them was a very pretty (because it satisfied my expectations) picture of growth, survival and reproduction rates as they related to the temperature and salinity gradients up and down the entire length of the river. They supported the notion that the Damariscotta is divided into three pretty distinct segments by natural factors, such as the major constrictions at Fort Island and Glidden Ledge, as well as depth, light penetration, and watershed contributions.

Oyster Farm in sight of Damariscotta

From the mouth to Fort Island is the river's ocean segment. From Fort Island to Glidden Ledge is the mid-estuary segment. Upriver from Glidden Ledge to the Damariscotta-Newcastle bridge and beyond is the upper estuary segment. Additionally, I was able to determine that the protected waters of the middle estuary (home to Maine's first commercial mussel farm) were every bit as suitable for artificial culture of this truly marine species as more exposed ocean sites would be. Indeed, that stretch of the river grew excellent quality mussels to market size in something like eighteen months.

Now, my home is about two miles above Glidden Ledge in the upper estuary. There are very few blue mussels on our shore, and if I want to gather mussels for dinner, I generally go downriver to Glidden Ledge or beyond where they're thick. Perplexingly, every year, I get heavy fouling of mussel spat on my float and moorings, and the question begs: Why no mussels on the shore?

Along the way, past the next green can buoy, is a ledge I call "Seal Rocks," a much-used haul-out for resident seals. A bit farther on begins the next section of the river, from Prentiss Cove to Glidden Ledge. It deepens from twenty feet in the channel to over eighty feet as you go. Prentiss Cove, protected by an island on the eastern side, is one of a number on the river that can't possibly be appreciated without being investigated, though it has a barrier ledge at its mouth and drains completely at low tide. It meanders way in until the river is no longer in sight, towering pines on both sides, and is a spot favored by clam diggers. There is a hidden cave, or used to be, where supposedly a murdering, renegade Indian hid from his pursuers until they found and shot him there. That's the story told to me by my cousin years ago. He wasn't sure of its veracity, but he showed me the cave in the side of a big, feldspar outcropping. The rock was all crumbling, and in the years since, the cave has diminished noticeably in size, and the only thing I have ever found in there is a phoebe's nest.

Because this cove is part of my immediate river neighborhood, I have spent a lot of time there, digging clams, duck hunting, checking it frequently for wildlife and simply enjoying its solitude. One of my favorite walks is out onto the winter ice there, where it is all fractured and jumbled around the edges and heaped on top of boulders in great, topsy-turvy piles with cakes four feet thick sometimes.

Catching the tide

An example of how the data from the experimental rafts explain this conundrum is that, despite heavy spatfall on XMR #9 (Crow Point, where I live), the growth rate of the older individual mussels that I measured each month at that site began to drop to noticeably less than the rates at sites farther downriver (especially below Glidden Ledge) in July and August. Meanwhile, by the end of September, there was a significant jump in the mortality rate of those same mussels, from 6% to 28% in just one month. By November (the end of the experiment season), mortality reached nearly 40%. The three rafts farther upriver saw this trend progressively amplified (with fewer and fewer spat, I might add, as well as greater and greater mortality). XMR#12 had 90% mortality by season's end.

What this all says is that while the early summer frenzy of growing and spawning might result in a good spatfall — kind of a flash in the pan — the overall year-round conditions with the higher summer temperatures and the lower (and seasonally fluctuating) salinities are just too stressful for this species to flourish here. Ribbed mussels, on the other hand, are an upper estuary species, as are oysters, and these do especially well in my part of the river – hence the present day profusion of oyster farms. And I have no complaints.

The Damariscotta is wonderfully varied. It exhibits gradients in many aspects. One thing is sure: it provides a wonderful environment for all manner of shellfish. When Ed Myers sent me to Spain on a fact-finding mission, I handed my card to a restaurant owner who looked at the word, "Damariscotta," and then bracketed the word "marisco" within, like so: DA [MARISCO] TTA. And then he said, " 'marisco.' That means 'shellfish'."

And I am not the only one who finds the place interesting – fox tracks zig-zag all over the place, especially around those piles where some morsel might be caught in the ice, and raccoon tracks, in the inner cove, shuffle between rare patches of exposed clam flats. The cove in winter is spectacularly beautiful – even otherworldly – and certainly bears no resemblance to the hot summer morning that finds me bent over the mudflat with a clam fork, horseflies biting my back.

A curious bit of information offered me by Kevin Scully, who has an oyster operation off the north end of Prentiss Island and who harvests his oysters by SCUBA diving, concerns what he described to me as a row (or rows) of wood posts in the bottom of his lease area there. That is pretty much the same spot where, at the outbreak of the War of 1812, the Walpole built, 400 ton ship *JANE* was scuttled to keep her out of the hands of the British – this according to Nelson W. Gamage in his *A Short History of South Bristol, Maine*. She was apparently raised again, after the war, "but her builder had much trouble in raising her successfully," all of which has me thinking they might very well have left something behind.

Eat Your Hearts Out
(partial letter to friends in Florida)

Let me tell you about yesterday morning. I went down to the shore as usual to check on things. It was still … whisper still. All the trees, most impressively the tall pines, were coated with pink and white hoarfrost, and the sun, which is a little higher these days, was beaming down through them with the bright promise of spring sometime in the not too distant future.

The river was royal blue with frozen trimming. Every once in a while, I could hear that sound like eggshells being crushed as drifting sheets of ice shaved over the rocks on the shore. Some old squaws were upriver somewhere, gabbling the way they do. Two gulls stood at the water's edge, waiting on the tide to bare the flats. Everything was bright white, green or blue … and sparkling like cut gems of every color.

I thought about your oranges and lemons and limes as I looked up into the frosted pines. I thought about your balmy, Gulf breeze as I listened to the stillness and the snow squeaking under my boots. And I thought, too, about bare feet and wearing shorts, the palm trees, chameleons in the bushes, alligators in the ditches, sand in the bed and all those Florida things that never change with the seasons.

Just then, though, I noticed something to bring my vision of Florida to its knees. On a hidden cue from the warming sun and in total silence, the pines overhead slowly released their clinging crystals of frost in an ethereal shower. The flakes drifted down around me so gently they seemed to float, each a tiny prism of rainbow light against the clear blue sky above. They filled the air, millions of them, everywhere, glittering, and not a sound. Can palm trees do that?

Prentiss Island

Blue Mists

I never count the days as summer wanes. The living's too good, too easy, to allow for that way of passing time. No, counting summer days is not something people should do, when it's much more soothing to forget what day it is altogether, to slip into that blissful swoon of timelessness measured only by sweeping oars and buttered ears of corn.

Instead, I count the layered hills that rest behind blue mists, and even then I'm not so careful about it, because how many there are is not important. What matters is only that there are so many colors, blue. There seems to be a shade for every hill, a blue for every distance, and what day it is hardly makes a difference.

I was standing on the shore, trying to point out a place downriver. My companion, taking in the view, was bemoaning his two weeks were nearly up, and he'd have to leave tomorrow. But he quickly abandoned such unthoughtly thoughts as he beheld the shades of blue.

"You see that darkest ridge," I said, "where the sun is beaming down? Well, look three hues farther on where the island's showing through the mist. Right along that shore is a damned good place to fish."

"You know?" he said. "Standing here, with summer all around, I'd rather forget what day it is and just count the colors, blue."

Next downriver is Hunter's Landing on the eastern shore, just north of Wiley Point, with a cluster of a dozen boats. Long ago (beginning possibly as early as the 1600s), it was a busy little harbor originally named McClure's Landing. Then, for a long period of time, it fell into disuse but has been revived and put to good use in recent years, an effort spearheaded by my friend Chester Rice who lives at this very spot and keeps his lobster boat there (and keeps us well supplied with lobsters I might add). According to him, this was very typical of the many clusters of humanity that occurred all up and down the river where the lay of the land and the depth of water suited. There was a wharf, built on stone-filled cribs, which provided a stop for river ferries, and there was apparently a good-sized store above it, near the old main road, and a number of houses. Next-door in the cove formed by Wiley Point was another of the numerous brickyards, a second wharf and a cradle for the shallow scows brought in on the tide and bottomed out for loading bricks. Hints of this still exist in the form of a few scraggly old apple trees that are a good indicator of old settlements. All such activity here being lost in a fuzzy history, today it is mostly limited to a host of gulls and terns lazing on the white ledges in the middle of the cove.

Across the way, on the west side of the river, is the Dodge Point Preserve with its two sand beaches, beautiful swimming and mile long shoreline, not to mention its 500 plus acres and several miles of trails. From the first moment this land was set aside for the public to enjoy, it has seen uninterrupted, year-round use on what I would deem a remarkable scale. Since we watch that shore from our kitchen table, I can attest to all the swimming parties, picnics, beachcombers, barking dogs, flickering fires in the night and, even at first light on the coldest mornings of the winter, those religiously regular hikers who emerge out of the woods in their bright red and yellow parkas. This preserve on the river, from my perspective, seems almost a temple where people flock to savor the river environment.

In the cove just upriver (part of the preserve), where a brook from a beaver pond empties out, are the remnants of one of the old brickyards. The scattered bricks on the shore make a rather nasty reception for small boat landings but at the same time are a rather curious and unexpected sight. Almost all the bricks are broken. If not, they are obvious rejects: twisted like wet sponges, cracked, bubbled, marred by handprints, and I once found one impressed with a dog's footprint, and another with that of a cat!

"Good Morning" from Glidden Ledge

27

Passing below Dodge Point's southern beach and Dodge Lower Cove, the river widens. On the same side, there's a funky little island that pops up out of the water like an inverted bowlful of rocky gravel. It's got some pretty big pines on it, one holding an osprey nest and another that has fallen in a graceful sweep onto the shore. Both sides of the river here, on close inspection, reveal old home sites, betrayed by scraggly apple trees perhaps, or by a pile of rocks, which might be the remnants of an old dock crib.

Before moving on, there are two curious things worth mentioning as we sit in the mid-river basin off Dodge Lower Cove. This is an area where gulls raft up or "roost" for the night. Many times on making my way home in the dark, even late into the wee hours, I have seen large flocks of these birds sitting on the water here. If my passing disturbs them, it's not for long; they quickly settle on the surface again. I'm not sure if it's a year-round roost, but one of the first signals of spring in late February or early March is the off and on, all night long cacophony of crying gulls we hear from our house. I presume they've got love on their minds.

The other thing of note at this spot in the river is on the bottom, or rather about ten feet under the bottom mud. It is an ancient oyster bed estimated by researchers to be nearly half a mile long and as much as ten feet deep. Several thousand years ago, the thinking goes, sea level was considerably lower than it is now, and therefore the Damariscotta, above the natural barrier of Glidden Ledge just downriver, was more a series of salt marshes than the tidal river of today. The species of oyster represented in the bed thrived in lower salinity water, and Glidden

Ledge effectively regulated the amount of salt water that flowed into the upper reaches of the river, thus enabling them to gain a foothold.

Approaching Glidden Ledge, the first major dividing point in the river separating the upper estuary portion of the river from the middle segment, the current begins to boil and churn and swirl. This very long and prominent ledge, with the tiny, poison ivy-covered islet at its eastern end, very nearly cuts the river off altogether. And if one watches a depth finder on passing through the western gap by the red day-beacon, it becomes obvious that there is a lot more to the ledge than meets the eye as the bottom line jumps up and down and spooky shapes begin to scroll across the screen. At the opposite end of the ledge, adorned by the little island, is a very narrow but passable gut. When the tide is running hard, it makes for a pretty squirrelly ride.

Apart from its interest to navigators, Glidden Ledge is a very interesting place in itself. Not only is a huge amount of water concentrated through this constriction in the river, but a huge amount of life as well, as is evidenced by bird activity at most stages of the tide and the regular presence of fishermen, not to mention the extensive beds of filter feeding mussels and all kinds of shellfish, starfish, urchins, anemones, worms and other invertebrates. Years ago, some friends and I found the downriver lee of the ledge to be a productive spot to dive for scallops, perhaps because of the number of sunken trees on the bottom that precluded any other method of gathering them. And I remember with great pleasure how good a scallop tasted, shucked and eaten with a heavenly, sweet infusion of salt water while still kneeling on the bottom, twenty feet down.

Shell Ice

I was eating breakfast. Out the kitchen window, stillness prevailed in the clear dawn except for the titmice and chickadees at the feeder. The river was placid, a coasting sheet of glass reflecting the far shore in the golden glow of first light. The tide had turned in the last hour, the boat on its mooring now headed upriver. The thermometer read eighteen degrees. Three buffleheads beat around the point and wheeled into the cove.

As I munched my toast, my eye caught some movement out there. The big red buoy on our mooring suddenly bobbed and jerked at the limit of its chain, and I quickly saw the reason as a thin glaze on the water's surface descended on the tide. And I knew what that meant, that the thin edge of winter was now upon us, and I would soon have to haul the boat out for the season

I took my coffee cup and stepped out on the stoop to listen, to listen for a sound I had not heard for some months, that of new shell ice knifing and chafing its way down the shore, slicing at everything in its path – a seemingly fragile force whose keen edge will soon sever all ties with warm weather and will lock the river up in winter.

My son, Elijah, fifteen years old and all woozled from sleep, stepped out to join me in his bare feet. "What're you doing, Dad?"

"Listen," I said. "Just listen."

And we did just that, for several long minutes. Our boat's fiberglass hull hollowed an echo in the quiet as the thin ice chewed at its waterline, and glassy, wet shells of crystal swished and ground around the ledges as sheet after sheet fractured and slid along with the tide. Elijah didn't say much, but he stood a long time in those bare feet, and I knew that this unexpected dimension of sound attending the phenomenon of shell ice was making an impression on him.

In my mind, shell ice will always be associated with duck hunting. A long time ago, on an early December morning, I sat on a point with my old cousin, Nape. He and I were regular hunting companions. It was cold and grey, and we sat brooding over a mess of black duck decoys from the driftwood and dried grass cover of our crude blind, freezing our asses off.

Nape was a tall thin man. He never wore gloves or mittens, and to this day I can see those long, bony fingers fumbling with red shot shells and the frozen, blued steel of his shotgun, and I can hear him grumbling about the madness of hunting ducks, leaving a wife and a warm bed to wade about in the freezing pre-dawn to set out a bunch of decoys and then to sit hours on a frozen rock in the vague hope that we had done something right and wouldn't get skunked. He loved duck hunting.

Anyhow, as we sat there, a great expanse of pure shell ice floated along our shore. We both watched in silence as this harbinger of seasonal change drifted into our consciousness. The edge of the ice then began to shred against the rocks at our feet, its fragile icy lens slicing at everything in its path. "Goddam shell ice," said Nape. "It's going to cut those decoy lines – I know it."

Never having seen that happen in my own lesser experience, I sincerely doubted him and said so. "It's just shell ice. It won't do anything."

"I'm telling you," he said. "Watch."

We watched … and listened. Soon the ice began to chuck away at the decoys. They yanked and bobbed on their green lines. I hoped the lead anchors would hold the bottom. The ice cut with a steady rhythm against the cork bodies. Some began to drag anchor. Then they all began to drag, or so it seemed. "See what I mean," said Nape. "I knew it!' And sure enough, it was soon apparent that several of the dozen decoys had been cut free and were drifting away with the ice. "Shell ice. It'll do it every time."

I scrambled for our canoe and paddled after them. Each decoy had just a few inches of frayed nylon string dangling from it. Not only did the sound of the canoe in the ice send every duck in the bay flying, we had to wait another couple of hours for the tide to drop so we could find the decoy anchors.

I've come to expect, on some early December morning, this signal moment brought on by the keen edge of the season's critical few degrees either side of freezing, when the first shell ice has formed overnight. It can make an impression on a young man. Locked in those fragile crystals is the hoarse whisper of things to come.

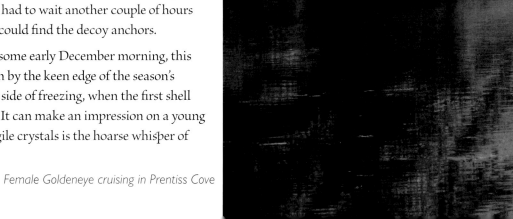

Female Goldeneye cruising in Prentiss Cove

As we continue southward toward Merry Island, which floats prettily in the middle of this narrow stretch of the river, we enter my old neighborhood where we lived on the Edgecomb shore for about sixteen years. On the right, or west, shore is a neat little pocket I call "Duffy's Cove", overhung on one side by old hemlocks. It leads up to what at one time used to be a good smelt brook in the spring.

Following along that shore, pretty soon appears a high cliff of a ledge, surmounted by a tidy house with rough-sawn siding, built by the same man who built the derelict schooner down below on the shore. The man was Robert Seefeld. The schooner, *Barbara Andrews*, after his wife, was built in Detroit back in the early fifties. Bob and Barbara decided to move to Maine, and in 1954 sailed across Lake Erie, down through the canal system to the Hudson River and up the east coast to the Damariscotta River, where they finally dropped anchor for good. They unloaded all their worldly goods on the shore and hauled them up through the woods to the same old farmhouse that my wife, Susan, and I eventually bought from them.

I commuted to work at the Darling Center by dory when we lived there, and I kept it on an off-haul tied to a big pine just up from the new Seefeld house on the cliff. One day on my return home, I was surprised to see Susan standing under that tree, waiting for me, and it was under that tree that she first told me we were soon to be parents – a happy moment in our life we will never forget.

Babe in the Woods

A lushness has settled on this river valley, a lushness of filled-out leaves and promising buds, of violets and bluets, and iris wedging forth from the deceptive flatness of their fog-green leaves. Nestsful of three and four eggs incubate under the fluffed breasts of sitting birds, poised under eaves, in thickets and secreted in the hollows of decaying trees. Blackflies and mosquitoes, succulent and swarming, emerge from the black, sphagnum pools of the brook in the woods, and, wherever I look or listen, there is an abundance of evidence that life and renewal are in the throes of passion. The river and the land around are heaving with life. They are a vast nursery.

In these woods, babes are born. And there are many. The moment of their beginning is one of wonder, nurture and tender initiation – one of perfection. But in the following days, that might not be so; there are also fear, competition and misfortune – the elements of natural selection. To live and thrive are more exception than rule, and the fate-dealing overlord is very much in attendance. Fragility and innocence are traits of weakness, not strength. Sweetness, sadly, is in the final assessment of the devourer.

Driving along our dirt road the other morning, I came around a green bend laced with ferns and splashes of dandelions. There ahead lay something dark and glistening. I slowed down to look but couldn't recognize it at first. It was not of these woods, it seemed. I stopped.

It was furry, about the size of a black cat – an infantile form, dead, slick with the morning damp. It had been partially eaten, but I knew by its form, its face, its clawed flippers, it was a baby seal. The shore of the cove was a good hundred yards from this spot, down through a steep, piney ravine. This innocent babe had not come here on its own.

Seal pups, it is well known, often become separated from their mothers. It is not at all unusual to hear them crying out mournfully this time of year. And such pitiful notes are sure to reach the ears of others, listening, who have babes of their own to feed. I suspected a fox, a regular in the neighborhood.

Had a fox heard this young seal? Sneaked up on it and watched for a while from the bank? Had she then dashed for it in a flash of orange,

grabbing for its chubby throat, yanked it, dragged it, bawling, up into the woods? That is what I imagined.

But such a heavy, struggling burden – it must have been a lot of work for the mother fox. Perhaps, on gaining the edge of the road, she had rested with the now lifeless pup and then begun devouring it where it lay. Or perhaps she had given up, frightened by a passing car. Maybe the torn flesh was the work of ravens or crows.

There was a particular sadness about this infant's lifeless body. We, in our idealism, don't accept such truths. This poor one had not only been lost by some quirk, but had surely suffered an undeserved terror at the end: abandonment, attack, bewilderment and pain. And then the final incongruity of this young seal's short life, to be dragged up and away from its appointed, sea level, environs into this strange world of pine trees and blackberry brambles by the side of our road. It made me wonder if our fates have ever been or will ever be anything but unexpected.

The dew-laden air was warm in the morning sun, almost hot. The sense of teeming life, and death, of the steaming wealth of new vegetation, and of milky breath, hung over this bend in the road, the last resting place of a babe in the woods.

Opening up across the river is Mears Cove between Lower Fitch and Kelsey Points. With its nice exposure, natural protection and out-flowing brook, this was once an ideal site for a brickyard. A good portion of it has a low-lying aspect and the look of land that, by its convenience to the river, has been lived on and worked for many generations. That notion was brought home to me one day when I was fishing for crabs as a small herd of lowing cattle slowly ambled along the shore there.

Then we have Merry Island, named after the old Merry family of ship builders and sea captains and happily populated in summer by close friends of ours and more than one pair of ospreys. There was a seasonal ferry landing where the present day dock is, to serve what I imagine was, in those days, a pretty active neighborhood that included a store up on the River Road. Touching the Edgecomb shore from low to mid tide, the island sits under quite a height of land in this narrow portion of the river, atop which is an old cemetery, and somewhere near it, we were always told, the remains of a Revolutionary Period gun emplacement to keep those darned British at bay.

Merry Island

It Waits for No Man

Down on the mudflats at low water, I am prone to contemplate the hugeness of the tide. The muck sucking at my boots squishes and squirms, acre upon acre of it, the primordial soup, loading the air to saturation with the black, organic smells of trillions of little lives beginning and ending in each moment.

I am actually standing on the bottom of the river. In six hours, this spot will be under ten feet of water. The black line on the rocks marks the level of high water. With little trouble, I can visualize the volume between shorelines that will soon be filled by the tidal surge … then emptied, then filled again, twice each day from this to eternity.

A "river" of water, half a mile or better wide, by twelve miles long, ten feet deep – that is the tidal exchange, something on the order of fifteen billion gallons of water in our river alone. And it is but one tiny finger's worth of the heaping bulge in our ocean that is pulled and tugged at by the seemingly distant Moon.

But who gives it much thought? The tide whispers and eddies past, hour by hour. The activities of birds, the digging of clams, the launching of boats – these are the things affected by the tides' rhythms. As the days of the year go by, the ebb and flow are measured merely by the little calendar on the kitchen wall … and not much else. Our interest is consumed by other matters. The quiet rise and fall of fifteen billion gallons of salt water elicits no more than passing, unexcited commentary, if any at all, so habituated are we to the influence and cadence of the heavenly bodies above.

But as I stand in my boots on the bottom of the river, I can't help but be awed by the colossal dimensions of the phenomenon that occurs in this place, and not merely once in a blue moon but two times in every day. The unimaginable forces at play, the immense volume of ocean water involved, and the implications of the scale of our planet's subjugation to the influence of near celestial bodies are what stop me in my tracks and make me think.

We have evolved with the tides' familiar pulse. So familiar is it that we have been lulled into a complacency of casual acceptance and the coining of quaint sayings like "Time and tide wait for no man." It occurs to me from my vantage point in the mud on the bottom of the river, if circumstances were a little different, if one or more of the planets were to be jarred into new positions and time and tide were goosed into "fast forward" somehow, say from the twelve hour cycle to twelve minutes, then I think we would see a more general appreciation for the ebb and flow we take for granted.

A six-minute flood (half of the twelve minute cycle) would be a true tidal wave of biblical proportions. The roar it would make, the havoc it would wreak on our coastline, would probably paralyze us with fear and admiration, and the general populace would certainly come to the trembling realization that the whispering tide with its gently swirling eddies is a phenomenon that merits something more than a quaint old adage. And it's a fair bet that philosophers like me wouldn't linger very long on the mudflats any more.

Off the south end of Merry Island is the charming islet, locally called "Mimsie's Island" – a clump of windswept pines, an osprey nest, very interesting rocks, perfect for a picnic (with the owners' permission).

The stretch along the eastern shore from there to the Darling Center on Wentworth Point is still as unspoiled as in the years when I twice daily made that run on my daily commute in my dory with its four horse motor. Those were blissful days, allowing me not only a rapturous solitude with my thoughts in all weathers, but the regular opportunity to dig clams or catch mackerel for supper on the trip home. I especially liked those passages shrouded in fog, the mother of solitude.

The western side of this portion of the river provides a selection of sights and places worthy of exploration. First is Salt Marsh Cove with its north and south branches. It is all mudflats at low tide, but a slow tour into the southern branch offers a visual feast of marbled ledges, huge overhanging hemlocks and glassy green water leading in to a very pretty and almost hidden salt marsh. It's the sort of place that makes you whisper.

Fox Chase

A friend and I went duck hunting one late November morning. A heavy dusting of snow had fallen during the night. Under a grey sky, in the black and white of winter, we paddled way back into the farther reaches of Salt Marsh Cove. It's a place where huge hemlocks hang heavily over high ledges along the shore to where a little reversing fall leads through an opening into a long grassy marsh. On our left was the tall, tree-covered rock formation that guards the opening.

A blue jay flew across the cove. We stopped paddling and drifted in silence, scanning the marsh for ducks. Suddenly, just in front of us, we heard the urgent sound of scrambling animals – had to be – up near the top of that rock formation. They seemed to be all over the place as branches dropped their fluff of snow and small rocks tumbled down to the water's edge. This went on for a good minute or two until suddenly, with a flash of orange, two foxes burst into view, completely oblivious of their audience. They chased each other up and down in what had all the appearances of a game of tag. And we just watched, our paddles resting on the gunnels. Such a pretty sight.

Then they saw us, two men in a canoe, in an instant of shocked surprise. In the next, they were gone, one shooting straight up over the rocks and through the trees, the other around the shingly shore and out of sight. Just like that, they evaporated.

Salt Marsh Cove

Coming out around the neck forming the cove, there's a succession of grand and gnarled old oaks. During the record rains in November, 1983, a number of them finally fell down over the shore when their great leaning weight became too much for the sodden soil, so it isn't quite as pretty there as it used to be. I know of one oak that year that slid, standing upright, about fifty feet down the bank! This is an ongoing process in many places up and down the river, whereby trees leaning out into the open for light are very gradually falling over, taking the soil with them and causing the shoreline to recede — an alarming, if natural, phenomenon.

Farther on is a small cove with several houses and an old wharf. This place was one of the old ferry stops called Poole's Landing. There were once a brickyard and an ice company here too, the ice operation being served by a small pond nearby. At the head of this cove is a gigantic rock, about sixty feet tall, that is undercut in such a way that it appears to me to be quite separate from any underlying bedrock.

Continuing on a southerly course, the Damariscotta now widens dramatically. Opposite Wentworth and McGuire Points on the east side, are Wadsworth, Burnham and then Pleasant Coves. Just south of the first two is a great string of ledges and boulders that wrap around the shallow waters of both coves. This is a fabulous place to get out and gather mussels and poke around. There's shell sand in places and lots of intertidal marine life to examine. In my experience, kids and dogs have no trouble entertaining themselves here, no trouble at all.

Human Industry on a Working River

The Damariscotta River has been no stranger to human industry in the recorded history of the last four hundred years. Fuzzy and mixed up as it is, that history has handed down to us the story of a "working river," a river whose aspects and abundant resources have productively supported human occupancy. The accounts we read in old diaries, ships' logs and in the many volumes written over the years

Salt Marsh Cove

important to us, of course, because it is OUR history, going back twenty generations. The existence of the oyster shell middens in Damariscotta and Newcastle, though, gives me far greater confidence in the historical accuracy of this notion that our river has been a "working river" down through the ages. The excavated record of human activity here, by various estimates, is thought to cover a span of at least 2000 years. Since native people were in this region as much as 12,000 years ago, I see no reason why the truth couldn't place people alongside the Damariscotta in the even more distant past.

There is a lot of mystery in connection with the early native cultures – the Red Paint People, Wawenocs, Abenakis and others – and how they lived. In the presence of such physical evidence as our celebrated shell middens, there can be no question that humans were here gathering and processing oysters on an industrial scale. And from excavations, we even know a little about the variety of their diet and eating habits, utensils and pottery, burial methods and such things. But beyond that, we have only tantalizing hints to keep us guessing at just what was going on. The mention of unearthed arrowheads whose geological origin appears to be in Ohio, the possibility of an active pearl trade and suggestions of cannibalism, all leave ample room for conjecture. The only thing we can be sure of is that they were here, and they were very busy. With imagination, a picture of ancient human occupation along the river's banks begins to take shape.

paint a rich and colorful picture of exploration, war and violence, great enterprise, and a cast of characters whose names are still familiar in our communities today.

But four hundred years is really not such a long time; the written historical record for this period only reflects the various activities of settlers recently arrived from Europe and elsewhere. It's

Then there's the relatively modern history of our last 400 years here. We know it was busy, but even still, much of our own story and many of its details have already been lost in the cobwebs of memory and vague record keeping. For instance, brickyards were once prominent and numerous along both banks of the river, and a flourishing brick-making industry not only supplied virtually all the bricks that built the town of Damariscotta, but was the basis of a burgeoning business that supplied this important building material to places as far flung as Boston and New Brunswick. Yet the names and locations of many of these yards have already receded from most people's memories, and much of the physical evidence of their ever having existed is largely hidden from view as they have become overgrown with trees and vegetation and eroded by the elements.

Though brick-making was a short-lived phenomenon on the river (40 or 50 years in the latter half of the 1800s), it is a good example of the "working river" offering up its resources in support of human occupation (in this case, marine clay deposits, fuel wood for firing the bricks, inflowing streams for needed fresh water and the river itself for transportation). Other archaic, riverine enterprises whose remains have largely disappeared from view included water-driven sawmills and gristmills, shipyards, ice companies and the many structures such as wharfs and quays that were needed to support them and similar operations.

The picture of the Damariscotta as a "working river" with a human presence is one that covers a great span of time – I think it's safe to say "aeons" – despite the many missing details. I only wish I could have been here to witness it at every stage from the beginning to now; I have so many questions. Today at least, we have our written histories and old photographs of more recent times, which give some satisfaction. To them I can add the archaeological survey made by Warren Riess and the late Nicholas Dean (of the Maritime Archaeological and Historical Research Institute) who (in 1988-1990) laboriously scoured every foot of both sides of the river for telling evidence of the past in order to chart the locations of any historic sites they found for study in the future.

The tally of what they uncovered, unsurprisingly, leans heavily in the direction of reinforcing the image of a "working river." It includes: 23 brickyards, 8 shipyards, 13 quays and stone wharfs, 4 mills, 2 ice companies, 2 lobster pounds, 2 dams, 1 salt works and 18 aboriginal sites (oyster and soft shell clam middens). Once again, the advantage of the river's rich diversity and resources is driven home to me as the underlying reason human industry has always been and will probably remain a major element in the character of the Damariscotta.

Pleasant Cove is just what its name implies. It is also the biggest diversion from the main river, extending a good 1¾ miles in the direction of Boothbay. A favored anchorage for cruising vessels, it is protected and beautiful. Having older houses with fields leading down to the water, numerous boats and a quiet atmosphere, it is an out-of-the-way river community. After the sharp bend southward about two-thirds of the distance in, the cove shallows considerably over extensive flats, but in a small boat at high water you can go all the way to the end to a rather wonderful, boulder-filled brook. On the way back out, on the right, is a nice little island, variously named "Muffie's" or "Huckleberry Island", where years ago we used to picnic a lot until "no trespassing" signs went up. On the east end of it, wide, smooth ledges slope very gently into the water, making for wonderful swimming.

Directly across the river next to the Darling Marine Research Center, is Lowes Cove, long and narrow, between Wentworth and McGuire points on the Walpole side. Other than the abandoned cabin at its mouth, the quiet remains of another of the old brickyards and a fallen-down duck blind, it feels untouched. The shoreline is low and gentle and lush with grass, the surrounding forest unbroken. A heron stands stock still like a solitary statue – it is another whispering place. This, like so many other of the choicest neighborhoods, has its resident ospreys with a magnificent nest.

Rounding McGuire Point, Miller Island lies in the middle of the river. Carlisle Island, west of it, has long been a favored camping spot, though I've never camped there myself. What I like is the high, steep Boothbay shoreline alongside it where I often ride very close in to admire the rocks and trees. A curious feature of this place is that if one stands on the island and shouts at the tall shore opposite, multiple echoes bounce repeatedly back and forth. This passage used to be a pretty productive spot for scallop diving too and might still be.

Way across from Carlisle Point is picturesque Clarks Cove, steeped in the history of its active role in the ice industry that thrived there. The picture painted for me is one of the huge ice house belonging to the Bristol Ice Company, that stored the ice cut on the nearby pond, and ships lined up to take on their loads for points south, even the Caribbean.

My experience in Clarks Cove, which was considerable when I worked at Ed Myers' commercial mussel farm, was mostly in connection to the then developing systems of aquaculture. Primarily, our mussels were grown attached to long ropes suspended vertically beneath various kinds of flotation, from old telephone poles to foam-filled tires to big plastic jugs – approximating the methods used in Spain, the world's leading producer of mussels. The ropes had short wood dowels skewered through them at intervals to keep the clumps of mussels from sliding down.

Clarks Cove

I remember in particular a hot August day when it was decided we needed, for future planning, a complete inventory of what quantity of marketable mussels were on hand. A friend and I put on our SCUBA gear and jumped in. We were under water for hours, estimating, float by float, what percentage of full capacity was growing on each. It was like swimming in an underwater forest among those loaded ropes (and they were loaded!) with its waving kelp fronds, nibbling fish, crabs and starfish. And on the bottom, where mussels had fallen, many more of the same scavengers were very actively cleaning things up, my favorites being the flounder, who were very curious about what we were up to, following us whenever we descended to their level. That was a most beautiful day.

I did get somewhat involved with ice in Clarks Cove, trying to break it up when winter's temperatures created enough to threaten the operation by dragging moorings and carrying things off. One night in a winter when the Coast Guard actually had to send an ice breaker up the Damariscotta, I got an urgent call to come help with shifting ice that was beginning to crush the boats against the docks. It was nearing midnight, 8° below zero and blowing. The ice was on the move and grinding hard. Ed and I were at it for hours with axes and push poles, but did eventually gain on the situation so that we thought we could let it go until morning. (Hell, it was morning! About 3:30 AM.) Finally able to relax the battle, I somehow managed to step backwards – right into the drink! Up to my armpits! The closest any human being ever came to metamorphosing into a polaris missile.

My Home River

My general use of the word "river" should not limit the reader's interpretation and imagination to thinking that by that term I'm referring merely to the wide ribbon of water that courses past. For me, this river is rather a superorganism, in the same sense as the school that sees planet Earth – the sum of all its parts, plant, animal and mineral, and the stabilizing interaction of all its natural systems – as one, large planetary organism.

Similarly, a "river," by rights, breaches the bookish definition by encompassing all that it influences, by throbbing with the pulse of its whole, by having its character manifested in the sum of its myriad biota, geologic structure, water flow, chemistry, seasons and moods. It is a living, breathing organism unto itself.

But I'm playing with definitions. I wade through this only to emphasize that this river place, once you've entered it, is a whole and separate world, self-contained, self-sustaining and all-encompassing, to include me and my way of life.

And I'm not alone. There's the bald eagle, sometimes with its mate, who regularly visits this point of ours. I look up and am suddenly aware of its huge, dark shape sitting in a big, old pine on the shore – still and silent and very much there.

And the eagle is not alone, for presently a crow shows up, abruptly landing and swaying on a dead branch. It, too, is silent … for a few moments at least … until it starts calling for the rest of its gang. Whereupon, their raucous and muscular assault on the intruder transforms our dignified eagle into a harried fugitive. After launching itself with a slow-falling, cascade of broken branches, it flaps determinedly for clear air space, veering sharply with every whooshing strafe by the crows. They hound the great bird relentlessly to the far shore and then leave off, satisfied they've rid the neighborhood of this riff-raff.

Crows are like that. One clear October afternoon, I was working on my roof and caught some motion out of the corner of my eye, down on the shore. The tide was out. Then I saw a low, dark shape scurrying among the rocks, checking out tide pools, poking into cracks, disappearing and reappearing in a methodical search for … what I wasn't sure – crabs maybe, or small eels. It was a mink. Pretty soon, unexpectedly, it surmounted a ledge and ran dead into a group of foraging crows, who, I don't have to tell you, got themselves pretty worked up over this intruder. They flapped themselves into a total frenzy, harassing the poor creature so thoroughly that it somersaulted repeatedly under their attacks to avoid being bonked on the head by a shiny, black beak. Crows think they own the place.

Cottages on Turnip Island, with Osprey Nest on Chimney

Sunrise, Lowes Cove

Mile by mile, the river is very much a collection of interacting communities of many different species. "Neighborhoods" is how I think of them, and they are made up of individuals with distinct personalities. Ospreys are a good example. When I used to work at the University of Maine's Darling Marine Center, I commuted by dory from my home near Merry Island on the Edgecomb shore. The green day-beacon just south of the island has for years been the nest platform for one or another family of ospreys. I say "one or another" because on my daily comings and goings, I observed very different behaviors from year to year in the parent birds, suggesting they were not the same individuals each season.

One year in particular, those ospreys made it their policy to not let a single cormorant wing downriver past their nest unmolested (at least not when I was watching). Time after time, I was witness to what must have been a highly traumatizing experience for the clueless cormorant who dared to barrel on down the pike too close.

One (or sometimes both) of the adult ospreys would instantly launch off its perch, either in a nearby tree or on the nest, and hurtle in the most menacing fashion after the cormorant, who, at the very last instant before being overtaken, would ditch into the water. Upon resurfacing and looking nervously about, it desperately tried to get airborne once more, whereupon the osprey(s) dove on it again … and again and again. I never saw a cormorant injured in these attacks, but this regular performance went on for weeks. The next year? Nothing of the kind.

Such bullying by ospreys has taken a new turn recently where I now live in Walpole. This time the regular victim is a great blue heron. Both birds are local to the neighborhood. I'll hear the most dreadful squawks coming from the cove by our island and, looking up from my weeding in the vegetable garden, spy the osprey repeatedly power-diving at a heron standing on the shore. With each dive, the heron ducks its head and clambers out of the way in the most inelegant manner. Finally, in desperation, the heron takes off in that slow, lumbering fashion that they do, only to be beset upon again by the osprey in what has the sound and appearance of being a pretty nasty business. Like the cormorants of years past, the heron

Progressing downriver from Clarks Cove toward the narrows at Fort Island, the east side is the more interesting course to take as it is broken up by several coves and islands and attractive sites with good anchorages, such as the little cove formed by a charming, high nubble some call "High Head". If the tide is up, I like to steer in around Peters Island a little farther on, where, for some reason, there often seem to be large rafts of mergansers and cormorants. (Something's going on behind that island.)

As I'm writing this, I feel compelled to comment on the uncommonly thick concentration of lobster pot buoys through this section of the river. They unquestionably constitute a hazard to navigation despite their stunningly colorful appearance when the sun is low and the surface like glass. But that they are there in such numbers, at a cost to the fishermen of say $75 apiece, is strong testimony to the productivity of the Damariscotta. It is also worth noting that this is the deepest section of the river with depths in places exceeding 100 feet. Continuing along the eastern shore, you enter Long Cove, shielded by Plummer Point. It is long and quite narrow, but of interest to me because of an extensive, steeply angled and perfectly flat rock face that is rather unusual on this river.

Ospreys in Christmas Cove

has no choice but to ditch. With those long legs and no webbed feet, this makes for a sad spectacle, the whole time the cove echoing with the heron's frantic calls. And of course my thoughts have to do with whether or not the heron will be able to lift its soggy self out of the drink. It does, clumsily, many times, only to be driven back down, over and over. Eventually, though, the osprey relents, and the poor heron labors off upriver like some battle-worn B29 retreating from hell. The only thing that seems to be at issue in these instances is territorialism. There is no food-robbing taking place. The trespassers appear simply to be getting on the ospreys' nerves.

Osprey nests seem to show a good deal of quirky variation as well. Typically, ospreys choose tall trees, navigational markers and elevated structures near the water for nesting sites. But I have seen nests built on house chimneys, boat docks and even right on the rocky shore, where one might walk right up to them. And although the nests themselves are generally recognizable, concave platforms of dead branches, some are pathetically under-built and falling apart (probably first year nesters) while others are masterful constructions of truly impressive dimensions, having been built up over many seasons. There is currently a nest in a big leaning pine downriver that must be six or seven feet tall. Eventually its growing weight will bring the tree down.

Ospreys are favorites among river watchers, partly because of their comeback in numbers after the scourge of DDT. But I think their presence on the river is a prime illustration of what gives the local neighborhood character. Their high-pitched raptor call, their spectacular fishing technique, their babies peering out of their nests, their watchful silhouettes perched in a dead snag and their

interaction with the rest of the river community – all these, to great effect, create the sense of place.

What is so rewarding to the observer is the rich variety in both animal and plant species in traveling the river, not to mention the varying heights of land, rock formations, shoreline and, of course, human habitations and settlements. These many neighborhoods that make up the river as a whole, while different, lend a coherence to this twelve mile riverine community that seems both brilliant in design and, from my appreciative perspective, providential. All the elements necessary to complete the picture of a healthy and beautiful tidal river are here, each playing its niche role, each adding to the marvelous complexity of the system and making it work.

It can be a line of ledges serving as a regular haul-out for resting seals, a place likely as well to be frequented by feeding gulls and cormorants and littered with their refuse of broken shells and the whitewash of their guano. Such a spot has mainly the character of a place used for loitering.

Main Street. Damariscotta

Then, in contrast, there are many parts of the river where the low tide shore is acre upon acre of mudflats. These are very busy places where many species (including man) work the flats hard for the even greater number of species of shellfish and other invertebrates that grow there – millions of little lives teeming with activity … and

Osprey nest in Lowes Cove

millions of deaths both sustaining the foragers and lending their remains to the rich, black muck and heavy, clamflat aroma. When the tide comes back in, so do striped bass and other foraging fish to take advantage of the disturbed flats. Of course the gulls and others are nearly always present, but if it is the season for spawning worms, for example, or migrating shoals of tiny herring, the surface activity over the flooded bounty becomes a great free-for-all of screaming and bickering birds, and I can well imagine some pretty energized stripers swirling just beneath their feet.

Where there are narrows and constrictions in the river, the current runs hard in boils and standing waves, surging around and over rock obstructions, scouring, mixing, flushing. The power of this tidal action is the most important force at work here in refreshing our estuarine environment and transporting planktonic organisms.

My point in all of this is that while there are distinct locations or even whole stretches along the river that have each their definable character, that stand out in my mind, they are like the rooms in a house – serving different functions and playing different roles in the lives within, but as a whole, they become a home.

I know where to go to gather oysters or mussels or to dig clams – all different places. I know where I am most likely to get a striper hit in the first few casts, a mysterious place where bubbles have for years risen up out of the muddy bottom, an oak ridge frequented by wild turkeys and where the coyotes yip and howl in the moonlight. I know where I can glide along a steep, brooding, forested shore, or find a secluded and quiet picnic spot with good swimming, or go to find a waterfall no one else seems to know about. I know where the eagles' nest is, downriver, and where huge hemlocks hang far out over steep ledges so a boat can ride in under them. And then there are communities of clustered houses and anchorages and the four villages of Damariscotta, Newcastle, South Bristol and East Boothbay with their active harbors and close ties to the river – boat building, marinas, fishing, aquaculture, light industry, restaurants and stores.

All these elements comprise the continuum called the Damariscotta River, my home river, which in itself is distinct from every other river in the world.

Around Plumber point comes first Farmers Island and then Hodgsons Island (called "Stratton Island" by many). The two straddle the mouth of Seal Cove, and, collectively, the islands and cove offer a trove of sights and hidden hideaways for picnics and swimming and inspirational subjects for at least two floating artists I know of. Years ago the view on entering the cove was marred somewhat by high overhead wires suspended from shore to shore between two towers (one with a big osprey nest on it, naturally). Their removal made all the difference in restoring the visual serenity of this place to its more natural state. Despite its popularity among recreational and cruising vessels; despite the frequent sport fishermen and the bird watchers, who sneak in to get a glimpse of the eagles nesting on Hodgsons Island; despite the measured increase of new homes built along the cove's eastern shore; Seal Cove still manifests a tenuous atmosphere of wildness, a preciousness that seems to hold a certain priority in river-goers' minds as a piece of the Damariscotta whose welfare must be guarded with great care. I could not agree more myself … but then I feel that way about the entire river.

A neat way to exit Seal Cove is through what they call the "Back Door" down in that neighborhood, the tight and shallow gap at the south end of Hodgsons Island. The first time, it's a good idea to scout it at mid-tide in a small boat to see just where the good water is as it winds around ledges and a shelly bar. It's a very pretty spot. Out in the river from there is a series of ledges, near which I recall some rather worthwhile scallop beds 25 or 30 years ago.

River Crossing

Along with the lengthy spell of cold weather that has descended on our woods has come a state of suspended animation. A week-old snowfall remains on the tree boughs. The deep pack lies trackless except around the house and at the foot of the hill where our neighbor, fox, crosses the road on his daily rounds. The river has ceased to move. Frozen over and covered with clean, windswept snow, it churns deep and dark and out of sight.

From out of the woods on the far shore, three timid forms emerge to stand at the beginning of the frozen expanse between us, to gaze over its distance and to yearn for something on the other side. Three deer, profiled against the depths of mid-winter rising behind them, contemplate an imagined wealth of browse up in my woods.

Hunger is their driver, hope their decision-maker, the frozen river, its strange open stillness, the source of their hesitation. Hunger and hope prevail though, and the three creatures negotiate the thick, tilted cakes of ice at the river's edge and soon find themselves out on it, where they are not at all accustomed to walking. Like children, they curiously explore the newness of their situation, sniffing at the saltwater ice where the wind has swept it clean, testing their footing and perhaps feeling a bit awed by the space around them and the novelty of their circumstance.

After a few minutes they venture forward, out toward the middle of the river where unseen currents swirl and heave just under their pointed, black hooves. The caution in their genes urges them on, not to linger in such a place. But they do not run. In single file, the three walk on, pausing only to lower their heads and smell the changing surface ahead.

Once, something unseen spooks them into a trot for twenty yards, but their caution renews itself. Just in front of them lies what looks like a large patch of rotten ice, weakened and honeycombed by the surging currents beneath. The three deer pause momentarily. They are more than halfway across the river now. My shore, the east shore, with all the lure of its unknown bounty, must seem very close. They look about, upriver and down. One of the deer turns and looks back over the route they have come, but the largest of the three, who appears to have shed his antlers, starts forward once more, and the others follow. They skirt the dark ice (much closer than I would have done), which they somehow recognize as menacing. And then, soon, they are faced with the reality of a new shore, more ice cakes jumbled by the tide and a steep bank, deep in snow.

I watch as the three make their way through the heaped, massive cakes, slipping and sliding, and gain the land. And then, with no hesitation, their strong haunches propel them up the bank overhung by low pine branches, and they disappear in a cascading cloud of powdery snow loosed by their arrival in my quiet woods.

All is still again, and cold, and except for the new set of tracks across the ice, nothing seems much different. A state of suspended animation, as I said, and continued bitter cold in the forecast, with more snow by the week's end.

Now we approach the final major constriction in the Damariscotta, the Fort Island narrows. There is tremendous current here when the tide is running – standing waves, whirlpools and boils galore driven by a volume of water on the order of 3400 cubic yards per second! In trying to visualize this, imagine it as the amount it would take to fill 283 dump trucks pouring through the narrows every second. That's a lot of water, and it represents just what is involved in the rise and fall of a ten-foot tide stretching ten miles farther upriver.

North of Fort Island is another "back door" of sorts that leads into the Back Narrows of East Boothbay. Because of the considerable current there as well as inconveniently placed rocks and ledges, I don't generally go that way except at slack water – maybe two or three times a season to check out the small harbor tucked behind the island. Besides, it is much more dramatic to shoot through the main narrows and the buoys marking the Eastern and Western ledges as we enter the ocean segment of the river and get the first glimpse of open water and the Atlantic.

By this point, one notices what I think can accurately be called a sea change – several, actually – all relating to the open, marine environment. There has been a steady, if subtle, progression of the forest type, from hardwoods and heavy mixed growth with lots of red oak and white pine upriver, to a predominance of softwoods, primarily spruce, the closer we get to the exposed coast. There is also the usual sharp drop in temperature (at least in summer) brought on by the colder ocean water, as well as a good chance of the sudden appearance of fog (where

"Witches Broom" just south of Fort Island

we had enjoyed clear, balmy weather an hour or so behind us). I find myself thinking, without needing to say out loud, "People, haul out your jackets. And feel the beginnings of an ocean swell. And quickly, on the left, note the huge 'witch's broom' in the top of that pine."

We have definitely arrived "downriver," and things are different. The water is noticeably clearer. The lobstering seems more in earnest as the pots are everywhere, with many buoys pulled under by the deep current, and lobster boats, each with its own cloud of gulls, ply and turn and charge all over the place. There are more and bigger boats of all descriptions as well. With a view of the open sea, not just the left shore and right shore, there is now an irrepressible awareness of an ocean world out there.

Leaving the East Boothbay shore for later, I usually keep to the South Bristol side to allow my companions to "house shop." Susan is particularly enamored of a big, white, many-dormered house, set back in an open field, with porches and gardens and apple trees (and, I can guess, an imaginary husband who will buy it for her, and a horse to go with it). I have several favorites along this stretch myself, including the spruce log cabin high on Jones Point, looking straight out to sea, and around in Jones Cove, the old Peterson place, which is one of the finest examples anywhere around of a salt water farm, including its boathouse on the stone wharf. But let us not get distracted; there are more good things to come.

Salt Water Farm, South Bristol

At this point the tour route hinges on a little "high seas democracy," as the captain asks for a vote on where everyone wants to go from here. Straight out to the islands? Damariscove? Little River, around the corner, if the surge at its mouth is not too rough? Or how about going over to Boothbay Harbor?

Chances are, no one has a clear opinion. They're too busy talking and eating sandwiches and resolve to leave it up to the captain, me, who has done a fine job so far of showing them the sights. And if there's one way I know of to get my passengers to pay a bit more attention to my river, it's to take them through the South Bristol Gut.

So I head over to the east side to The Gut, which is the passage that slices Rutherford Island off the tip of the South Bristol peninsula. And it quickly becomes apparent that this is the business end of the Damariscotta River as the village of South Bristol presents itself, full view, with its close-set houses and waterfront buildings, some with red roofs, others with roofs sporting rows of sea gulls and most with some semblance of a dock or wharf set on a forest of pilings. There are a lot of weathered wood shingles, piled gear and traps, plenty of boats and a dragger or two.

Half Moon Cove

On the left is the famous Gamage Shipyard, in its later years a collection of big, old sheds with sagging profiles, tattered shingles and broken windows – so ugly they're beautiful. But of course it's the history of this yard and the pride and attachment its community has for it that makes it "beautiful" in their memories – sending down its ways, time and again, vessels with such well known names as *Shenandoah, Bill of Rights*, Pete Seeger's *Clearwater* and *Hero*. Today the old place is being transformed. The dangerously "ugly" buildings are being torn down, one by one, while a handsome new boatyard and marina is growing in their stead with a mind to preserve what history it can.

Still, it's certainly not quite what the old place used to be, according to my good friend, Bruce Farrin, who worked nearly ten years in the Gamage yard before starting up his own boatshop across the way on Rutherford Island. His experience of growing up around boats in The Gut, asking questions and making a nuisance of himself in old Sumner McFarland's boatshop as a kid, then going to work in the Gamage Shipyard, eventually to become a ship's joiner, is as good an example as any of how Maine's shipbuilding tradition has been nurtured down through the generations. It represents a life of hard work, hard lessons, hard-earned reputation and deep pride.

Seal Cove

Meditation Spots

There's this thing that people do here. They sit, and watch, and stare, and think … and, no other way to describe it really, they just quietly luxuriate in the peace and beauty of their surroundings. And I don't recall ever seeing more evidence of this phenomenon than I have up and down the entire length of this river.

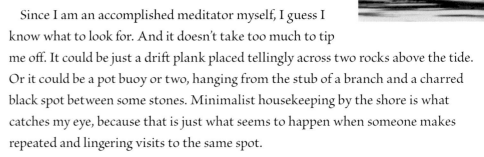

Since I am an accomplished meditator myself, I guess I know what to look for. And it doesn't take too much to tip me off. It could be just a drift plank placed tellingly across two rocks above the tide. Or it could be a pot buoy or two, hanging from the stub of a branch and a charred black spot between some stones. Minimalist housekeeping by the shore is what catches my eye, because that is just what seems to happen when someone makes repeated and lingering visits to the same spot.

The variety of form of meditation spots makes me smile. They're as varied as human beings themselves and their disparate ideas of what it takes to be contented and comfortable in the setting of their thoughtful interludes. I see the simple planks; I see wooden cable spools, Adirondack chairs, plastic chairs, half-log benches, iron park benches, love seats, all manner of tables, hammocks of string netting or striped canvas, Buddha statues, Mexican fireplaces, potted geraniums and flags.

Lobster trap buoys in the early morning sun

Many of these spots are in surprising places. I suppose that's because no house is in sight. But on thinking about it, that makes sense; being away from things, the parishioners, or whatever you call them, can find true solitude. Some, indeed, are in hard-to-get-to locations, which suggests to me they see only occasional use. But the common denominator is proximity to the river, where soul-searching and soul-soothing are part of the landscape.

I personally have six meditation spots, not counting my boat or the kitchen table. I frequent them all, but I have my favorite out in the pine grove by the shore where there is a round, wooden table and chairs and a heavy bench by a big stone fireplace. I use it year-round. My preferred hours are sunset or dawn, when the light is poetic and the air is still. And though I don't really have a favorite season, I'm especially happy on an autumn evening with a fire going, its blue pine smoke drifting out over the river, a drink on the bench beside me, maybe something to munch on, and my dog leaning against my leg, hoping for a handout. I just sit and watch and listen, lost in my thoughts. And time stops.

A Buddha overlooks Salt Marsh Cove

To wit – Just seven years after starting his own boat-building business, Bruce's entire shop, most of his tools and a half-completed wooden hull, were swept wholesale off the wharf where they stood by the huge ocean storm of February, 1978 – a total loss; within a few days he began construction of a new shop and was soon back in business, to become one of the most highly regarded lobster and pleasure boat builders on the coast today.

Straight ahead past Gamage's, almost like a banner, hangs a single span of power lines to the island, and under it, the short, green swing-bridge, hard to see as it is kind of jambed between buildings. Three toots of the horn eventually get some response from the bridge keeper, and, with flashing yellow lights, traffic stops and the bridge swings slowly open.

And this is the part I like … all the jabbering and sandwich munching suddenly ceases as we slip through the narrow opening into South Bristol's beautifully secluded little harbor in The Gut. Before us, all around us, is a feast of lobster boats, bigger fishing boats, draggers, a work barge or two, Friendship sloops, company buildings and houses climbing the hillside, wharf after wharf piled with traps and buoys, a mackerel weathervane on the right, kids zooming about in a skiff, two eyesful of colorful boats with inspiring names, the noises and voices of waterfront industry, busy fuel docks and a steady rhythm of activity at the Fishermen's Co-op. It's almost more visual stimulation than my companions can stand, as several of them declare a sudden need to go to the bathroom. I head for the Co-op to buy fuel and to avail my stricken crew of the fine plastic outhouse there.

"Fleetwood"

Towing a Work Barge

Gamage Shipyard

Washing the dock at the co-op

A family fishing at the co-op, Gem Island in the background

The Old Woman's Breath

Two nights ago the old woman in the river finally froze. At last the river's surface is motionless except for the heaving and cracking of its edges on the tides. I feel as though I've written this piece before; there is a familiarity to it. Each year with the renewal of that cold and still expanse, I am inspired to acknowledge, one more time, this amazing manifestation of the planet's pulse and the enormous implications it has in connection to the ebb and flow of the earth's energy budget.

I think there are times when my wife wants to hammer me on the head with a giant mallet, as when I stand at the bedroom the window in the moonlight, expounding on the eerie beauty of this frozen river that beckons me to join it in the winter night. I can't help myself. There is a stillness and a glow, deceptive it's true, that lure the insomniac into a complacent trance that can only be ascribed to a touch of moonlight insanity. As the moth is drawn to the flame, I want to go there.

On looking downriver a mile or so, I can see an open patch of water and the old woman's breath steaming in the night, gently, as there is no wind, just barely perceptible wisps of vapor in the cold air. Her great age and (I am reminded) long experience in these wintry matters are, for her, but dreamy echoes of ice ages in the past. The stones and pebbles and chunks of sod gripped in her bony fingers along the shore are mere mementos of the passions she's known over the eons of time, when earth and bedrock yielded to her whims and when the breath of winter enveloped the hemisphere.

In our relatively brief winters, we comfort-seekers are spared long periods of coping, yes, but if we are to gain any true sense of the huge elemental interactions that can bind a whole river in ice, thaw it out and freeze it again, a million times, to scour the land and shape it, boulder by boulder, grind it down until it is but the finest clay in the river's bottom, I think we must depend heavily on our imaginations and what volumes of science there are on the library's shelves. It is a long and unending business that I ponder in the moonlight.

What might it be like to live and grow up in the rich environment of this little corner of the world? Again, my friend Bruce Farrin can help to paint that picture as it was half a century ago. In discussions with him and his cousin, Ronald House, a quaint image of their youth takes shape, and I see boys not much more than 10 or 12 years old hauling their few lobster traps (maybe 20) right there in the harbor and only just so far outside The Gut in either direction, that older folks could keep an eye on them – no farther than Jones Cove in the river, no farther than Gem and Witch Islands going out the other way into John's Bay. They describe a great fear of the river, its currents and sucking whirlpools, among the mothers, aunts and grandmothers in their lives, a fear perhaps stemming from the not-so-long-ago times of frequent shipwrecks and drownings on the coast.

But that didn't keep the kids off the water. Young girls worked in the sterns of their fathers' lobster boats and went periwinkling and mackerel fishing, as well as taking the usual storekeeping and nanny jobs. The boys, besides lobstering, set gillnets for alewives there in the harbor, by the bridge and out by Webbers Ledge in front of the Gamage Shipyard, netting maybe a couple of bushels and selling them for bait, getting as much as 10 cents apiece. And sometimes they helped the older men tend their mackerel traps outside at Thrumcap Island and over at Pemaquid. Through high school, Bruce (and, I imagine, kids like him) expanded his lobstering farther afield to include 75 to 100 traps, fishing them out and around Rutherford Island and into the Thread of Life, which is where my tour takes us next.

Dawn of the Longest Day

Four o'clock, the crack of dawn … what a magnificent hour! I don't mean the grey dawn, when the silhouettes of the trees slowy take shape within the frame of my window. I don't mean the weakly creeping, salmon-tinged sky, ushering in "just another day." No, I mean the crack of a summer dawn when the longest days of the year fairly fly in out of the northwest – the white clouds outlined with pink and slate, the cool morning air rippling the surface of the river – like a muscular painting that exclaims, "What a fine Maine day this is going to be!"

It is only just after four, and already I see the hummingbird perched on the old iron hoop that holds its feeder. From the shore with my first cup of coffee in my hand, I can look far upriver and down, two or three miles, and see the first boats moving about and hear the whine of a clam digger's skiff coming down to catch the tide. And I think to myself, if only we could have such a bright and early dawn every day of the year. And I remember the song,

"Summertime, and the Living is Easy."

Exiting the east side of The Gut for the trip around Rutherford Island, we head into Johns Bay, bounded on the far side by Pemaquid Neck. While technically not part of the Damariscotta River, this is the route I generally follow; it is very scenic and offers a distant glimpse of the old stone fort, Fort William Henry, at the mouth of Pemaquid Harbor, plus a "real time" perspective of that historically important peninsula. Better than that, perhaps, is the likelihood of a good "sleigh ride" on the sea swells that usually roll into the bay.

In places, along this eastern side of Rutherford Island, I'm inclined, at low to mid-tide, to steer close to the rocks to admire through the crystal clear water the beautiful rusty-green of the Irish moss that grows along there. I've often thought that would make a great color for the hull of a boat named *Rockweed*.

At this juncture, however, my aim is to take us on down to the south end of the island. It's a straight shot past the landmark eighty-foot, wooden tower on the old Miles estate and Birch and Hay Islands. Chances are, there is some pretty good surf and wave action along this shore as it is wide open to the incoming swells. And if that's the case, the string of high ledges from Crow Island to Thrumcap usually puts on a pretty good show of exploding white spray, punctuated here and there by heaving, glass green surges and long rafts of eiders. By cutting in between the nun and can buoys just north of Crow Island to rejoin the Damariscotta at its mouth, we enter the protected passage flanked by those ledges and Shipley Point at the tip of Rutherford Island.

The "Louise B.", a new tug built by Dick Shew and Cecil Burnham

Lobstering in the Thread of Life

This is known as the Thread of Life, a wonderfully scenic spot with an appropriate name – this place is loaded with life. It has some of the most beautiful underwater scenery I have ever seen. The visibility is exceptional. The rocky bottom near shore is a paradise of algae, fish, crabs, urchins and lobsters, everywhere, peeking out of crannies. I did a fair bit of diving there at one time and found a huge boulder, maybe 10 or 15 feet tall, completely covered with brilliant, emerald-green sea lettuce – an absolutely stupendous sight!

On surfacing beside that rock, I could look right up at a little, shingled house nestled among the spruces atop the high ledges onshore – the very house once occupied by Hilda Hamlin, the real-life "Lupine Lady" credited with spreading, far and wide, the seeds of that much admired flower. Yes, the Thread of Life is a real treat for the eyes, including those of the gangs of gulls and cormorants, holding their wings outstretched to dry, who lounge on the white ledges that lead out to Thrumcap Island.

Thrumcap's southern knob has a nice, protected little hook of a cove, spanned by a sandy beach. It's a great place for swimming and picnics, but a little too popular for my taste. The last time I was there, four boatloads of like-minded folks came in and landed right beside us with disgruntled looks on their faces, as though each expected to have the place to themselves. The world is still big enough to find private quietude; on that occasion we left.

From Thrumcap, there's always the temptation of the islands farther out, each a world in itself. I am particularly fond of the White Islands, their bold, wave-washed, bare, white profiles lurching out of the sea; a lonely chimney (all that's left of a house that burned) testifying to the romantic lunacy of someone's attempt to domesticate them; the resident bird colonies who claim it for their own. Damariscove and Fisherman Islands, in elongated grandeur, have their well-documented histories of domestication on the other hand. They are places where many people have spent much of their lives. Each of these two has its separate charms, one of my favorites being the little cove on the east side of Fisherman, cobbled with some of the most beautiful stones I have ever laid eyes on and where swimming becomes an act of baptism. Those islands, including Inner and Outer Heron Islands, are the geological extensions of the South Bristol peninsula and East Boothbay's Linekin Neck. In that sense, they are the seaward sentinels of the Damariscotta River.

But on this tour, we head back into the river proper. Having seen the fine example of a fishing harbor back in The Gut, I next like to give my companions a little rubber-necking experience in Christmas Cove's yacht harbor, which is nicely situated for coasting sailors on the southern quarter of Rutherford Island. It is surrounded by closely spaced houses with enviable views and plenty to look at.

*Turnip Island with Thrumcap in the background
from the very end of Rutherford Island*

The Gut, South Bristol

My impulsive crew, having eaten just about all of the lunch items, having momentarily lapsed in their noisy conversation, and, having already gone through their "house-shopping" routine, they suddenly launch into a furious binge of "boat-shopping" as we enter the yacht basin, passing between the two day-beacons (one of which, yes, has an osprey nest on it) at the entrance. No surprise – a place like this has many pretty boats, and in this case, many of them are rather old and immaculately kept. The kids always go for the fast-looking boats. Dreamers generally lean toward the more expensive. Me? I kind of like the beautiful old lapstrake, double-ended lifeboat, white with dark, green trim, that's moored way in the back end of the cove.

Christmas Cove, not unlike many similarly favored communities on the Maine coast, has a layered history, sort of like sedimentary rock, whereby its composition, and atmosphere I suppose, has built up over many generations with new "material" that has drifted in from many sources. At one time, it couldn't have been much different from any other natural, protected cove convenient to the sea – a good fishing harbor, a handy stop for coastal schooners and ferries, and, because of its friendly geography, the obvious place for a working community to grow and thrive.

Approaching the swing bridge from the western Gut.

Miller Island

Indian Summer

All through a week of cold, raw rain, I reacquainted myself with autumn's menu, printed on soggy leaves on the soft and sodden ground. I heard the blustering wind tearing through the trees in the night, stripping off their colors, snapping branches and in general wreaking havoc all around. I thought, better get some wood in; better get the cradle ready to put the boat to bed; better think about the snow plow.

There've been lots of ducks trading up and down the river, careening in and out of coves. Great floating swirls of leaves and needles meander on the currents' eddies, and as I watched a pair of herons the other night, flapping in slow-motion and croaking their way downriver in the falling darkness, I said out loud, "You two better get those long, skinny legs out of here pretty soon. If I were you, I'd head south."

And then ... the weather softened. The winds died off. The sun came out. And summer returned, or so it seemed, for a glorious encore – a fond farewell perhaps, a caress in parting, to let us know she will be there, waiting, on the other side of our orbit.

It was surely the finest of Indian summers, one whose grandeur was not lost on a soul, certainly not me.

By the time the sun rose high on October's last Sunday morning, I was gone. There was nothing left of my resolve to make the most of such perfect work weather, nothing but a little white dinghy, left behind, swinging on the mooring.

73

Perhaps because of its more attractive attributes, as the generations evolved who had a little more leisure time on their hands, Christmas Cove gradually became a destination for summer vacationers seeking the sea air and pristine beauty of a place with a growing holiday reputation and the name to go with it. My wife's grandfather, Frank McIntosh, a hardworking man who owned and ran the Needham Ice Company in Massachusetts, never took a vacation or went anywhere in his whole life … except once. Where did he go? Christmas Cove in South Bristol, Maine. Maybe he came on ice business, but I don't think so – on his post card to his intended, Miss Elzie Mae Horne, dated July 28, 1901, he wrote, "It's raining a little and we have to stay in camp. I haven't seen a girl now for four days. Have been living on lobsters and blueberries for the last two or three days. We're going to have some saltwater eels tomorrow. You get postage stamps up here at the same store as you do salt pork." He also brought away with him a gift for her, a teacup with "Christmas Cove, South Bristol, Maine" and a picture of the Summit House on it.

The changes didn't happen overnight. People born in "The Cove" hung onto their properties, and some still do. And there are plenty around today who well remember earlier periods of the transition from working community to summer community. In any event, it certainly has stayed vibrant despite a slight air of exclusivity. And most importantly, positioned as it is at the mouth of the river, poised on the edge of the Atlantic, Christmas Cove is very much in the grip of those forces and phenomena that most steadfastly define it.

Christmas Cove

"Vandy"

A Summer House (letter to friends)

I am spurred to write after having paid a visit to your cottage on the island the day after the last storm. From a distance, I could see the island was glazed with a low tide icing around the shore, and as I approached, a good northwest breeze lofted great clouds of snow out of the trees and over the water, like a shimmering fog bank in the sun. The ospreys wouldn't have recognized their nest of sticks, now no more than a huge cupcake on a pole.

I climbed the shore up over heaped slabs of ice, everywhere pale blue and dripping, and strapped on my snowshoes. As always, the door on the little shack by the dock hung open. The robin's egg interior was as warm with winter's glow as the broken wicker chair still propped outside, a snowy pillow on its seat, and I shuffled on up to the house over the tops of waist-high firs.

A great snowdrift encircled the place, piled there by the wind off the water as it whistled around the back shed and the porch. The house itself sat in a bowl only inches deep by the foundation, yet four feet high on the rim, and this curling dune swept precisely up to the front door, where it sifted through the screen mesh onto the porch and dusted the wood box and the windowsills.

I went around back. Everything looked restful through the windowpanes. September's calendar hung on the wall within. Five tattered, leather-bound volumes of the *Century Dictionary and Encyclopedia* idled on the bookshelf alongside Jack London's *Call of the Wild*. Below, on the bottom shelf, a pile of jigsaw puzzles lay fading in the early afternoon sun, and I wondered how many winters they'd passed that way, paling a little more each season.

By the kitchen sink, the dish rack sat nearly empty except for a cup and a spoon and a dishrag hung over the side. On the Franklin stove was a scallop shell. Everything looked in order and as you must have seen it, glancing back as you locked the door.

Eastern Gut

I was satisfied that all was fine, if a little lonely in your absence, and I left as I had come, shuffling over the tops of waist-high firs on my snowshoes.

We all await your return.

One of the more memorable events in recent times was the same February howler of 1978, referred to earlier, that bore into "The Cove" and gave the place a thrashing folks had not seen the likes of in quite a stretch of years. That southerly, with huge tides and heavy swells, blew right in over the barrier ledge and islet at the day-beacons and tore the place up. A cottage with a stone foundation was walloped so hard it was thrown 18 feet back on the shore. The Coveside Inn and Marina got hit the worst; the docks were demolished and the restaurant utterly destroyed. An uncommon event in any one lifetime, this sort of thing is still an ever-present, if rare, character trait of the river to be counted on to rear its head from time to time.

Another unusual natural phenomenon to afflict Christmas Cove, indeed, almost the entire river, for two or three summers around 1990, was the remarkable series of pogy die-offs that struck the coast. Driven into rivers, embayments and harbors by bluefish, the pogies were often so thick that it seemed one could just step out of his boat and walk on them. I remember my sister's comment that she felt she was witnessing something out of the bible.

I have in my mind's eye the vision of massive feeding frenzies that played out over vast areas: screaming, bickering gulls and terns circling overhead, fighting and splashing on the water; cormorants by the dozen, diving, then resurfacing to gulp down their prizes snatched from the swirling and panicked, schools of golden fish; gluttonous seals, viciously charging into the melee; the bluefish, murderous, slashing, sending chunks and pieces of pogy into the air; and the noise it all made, like strong rapids in a stream.

To Soar or to Hurtle?

An autumn afternoon lazing downriver, in my mind, is one of life's more soothing occupations. It requires nothing more of me than a simple laying down of tools and the happy abandonment of chores and less pressing matters. These I leave to September's forgiving spirit; she is generous with her afternoons and is quite convincing that October's calendar will leave enough time for such things.

And so I was seduced by September's last Saturday to make the most of its fresh, southwest breeze playing against a full moon tide. A man in East Boothbay had called me to have a look at an old, hollow, apple tree. He heard I was looking for one. He wanted it removed; I could have the wood for the taking. As good an excuse as I needed, I dropped everything and headed for the shore.

The elements conspired toward perfection … bright blue sky, flying white clouds, silver chop against green water, a warm friendly wind. I think it was the dazzling, afternoon sparkle on the water that got me, calling me to come hither, to leave the chores behind. And I did. It was such a handsome day, I seized it before it got away.

After a leisurely ride downriver, I met my friend at his dock. He took me to see the apple tree. We made arrangements, and I got back aboard my boat. There were no other errands, no time constraints, nothing more I had to do than spend the rest of the day as I saw fit.

The tide was unusually low, bringing to light certain things in the river I don't ordinarily see – deep rocks and ledges with glistening kelp fronds waving in the breeze, an oyster bed just below the surface, a sunken oak tree. Great blue herons stood poised and watchful every few hundred yards, making the most of the exceptional tide, and everywhere, it seemed, gulls worked the flats like gangs of itinerant field hands.

I took a good amount of time poking along the shore, looking for interesting things to salvage, enjoying the extravagance of the long afternoon, stolen and now mine. But at last, I realized I must head for home.

Halfway upriver, I saw a great bird wheeling high over the tree tops along the shore – a bald eagle – large square wings, white head, white tail. Without effort, it hung in the September afternoon sky, free and unconcerned, and my spirit soared with it. Yet I knew, too, my own soaring would soon end with the coming press of October's colors and crisp air.

And then another vision visited me. A large, plump, brown bird drove out hard from the shore. It was a partridge, headed across the river, which was nearly a mile wide at that point. It pumped its wings with a fury, hurtling across my bow like a feathered cannon ball, glided, then pumped, glided and pumped, with what seemed a fantastically desperate effort for so fat a bird with such stubby wings.

"October's partridge," I thought, as it hurtled past and into the distance, where it finally gained the far shore to swoop into a grove of ancient oaks. I continued upriver, reflecting. To soar or to hurtle? It seemed the time for soaring was slipping away with the last of September, while the need to hurtle would soon be fast upon us.

There were so many of the dead, oily fish, they looked like autumn leaves spread over the water for miles. The stench was unbearable. The slime covered everything on the shore, including docks, boats, even lines dangling overboard, and it lasted into the following spring, killing the sea lavender. Christmas Cove fared better than most through this trial, probably because of the proximity to the open sea and its flushing action, but the harbor, enclosed as it is, saw impressive millions of desperate pogies corralled in its confines, gasping for air at the surface of the oxygen-depleted water and being driven up onto the rocks.

In large part, what people have to say about life at the far end of the river is more benign, though the picture painted has its distinctions. The climate is a bit different for example. In spring, the still-raw temperatures pretty much keep the black flies to a minimum. In summer, that end of the river might be in thick fog all day under the influence of the colder ocean water, whereas Damariscotta and Newcastle are finding it hot and sunny. And it is not at all uncommon during a winter inclemency for it to be raining in Christmas Cove (under the relatively warm marine influence in that season), sleeting in Walpole and Edgecomb, and snowing heavily at the upper end in the twin villages.

A nervous group of young Eiders

The French family were long time residents in "The Cove". A conversation with Jack French, recalling days spent with his father, Louis, jigging for cod by the boatload just outside at Inner Heron Island, points to another difference between upriver and down. A boy fishing just a bit farther upriver probably wouldn't have caught any cod at all, but rather mackerel or stripers or flounder.

Other anecdotes involve old Joe French, Jack's grandfather from Christmas Cove, who seems to have tried his hand at just about everything the Cove life had to throw at him there on the edge of the sea. His was very much a maritime existence. While he worked for a time at Rice Brothers Shipyard in East Boothbay, up and over on the other side of the river, he rowed back and forth in a dory through what I well know can often be a nasty stretch of water at the mouth with a strong tide against the wind. He also spent periods around 1900 living out on Damariscove Island, handlining and lobstering in his rowboat and commuting from there to Christmas Cove in a small sailboat.

One of old Joe French's more memorable endeavors apparently took place during one very cold, long ago winter (1909-1910) when the Damariscotta froze solid all the way out at least as far as Inner Heron Island. Joe was doing some carpentry work out there that year. Once the boats were locked in ice in the harbor, it seems he had little alternative but to walk to the island and back each day, hauling his toolbox behind him on a sled! It's quite an image.

Leaving the Gut for a days work.

Before leaving Christmas Cove, there is one more image that paints this place as something more than meets the eye, not merely a charming cove community at the end of the river. It is that of a man standing atop a short ladder leaned up against the wooden cistern beside his house. Looking left, then right, he hoists something up out of what one would expect was his household water supply. Then, with the tinkling sound of glass bottles, the man climbs down and hustles around to the back door. Various accounts of similar odd goings-on come from several sources. Sometimes the ladder is leaned against the house itself, and the man is reaching into the roof gutter. Other times it's just an old hollow apple tree.

Maine was the first state in the nation to adopt a prohibition law in 1851, so I suppose this scene could have played out any time between then and the end of Federal Prohibition (1920-1933). In the bottles was bootleg liquor, obviously. And Christmas Cove's dirty little secret was that, being so close upon the regular coastal trading route and not known for resisting temptation, it couldn't help but become another in what was probably an extensive network of friendly harbors for bootleg smugglers.

I look to my tour companions and say, "Let's get out of this place. The day's getting on. We'd better be thinking about getting back. I've got a little more to show you." Rounding Foster Point, and heading upriver, we pass the spot where my five year old son, Elijah, hooked his first mackerel … got so excited, he threw his arms up in the air …and rod, reel, the whole rig, went overboard!

Tenuous Beginnings

I am often struck by how birds will nest in the most perilous situations, just inches from danger, their whereabouts concealed by only the flimsiest camouflage, or in the case of some, none at all. Indeed, it would seem that birds, in general, are drawn to the brink of potential disaster as if that were the essential ingredient of the wild, free spirit that keeps them flying in the face of even the most threatening elements.

I can imagine a higher purpose in all of this; by exposing their most vulnerable side to the forces of natural selection, they are thus ensuring that only the most worthy of their specie will launch themselves from the rim of the nest to experience the thrill of life.

One November day, I went off with a friend after sea ducks. Few creatures on Earth are more exposed to raw, elemental nature than sea birds are, and yet these tireless mariners are so well adapted to their existence that they would seem to bathe in even its most extreme conditions of cold and wind and hissing waves. The more terrible the weather, the more they appear to luxuriate in it, stretching across the grey horizon in long, low-flying lines by the hundreds.

In pursuit of some action, we landed at a high, bald mound of granite that rides uneasily in forever surging seas. It is a place that sea birds love, and I found myself climbing on all fours to gain the top and look around. Completely exposed to wind and ocean, the only possible protection might be found in a crevice or two, for a few hours' time, but even they would be scoured in every tide. An unseemly place for eggshells and babies, yet here and there among the few tattered tufts of grass, was evidence that birds had nested there.

Flattened on the guano-stained rock were the remains of crudely built gulls' nests (which are only rudimentary at best). About their shallow depressions, broken shells of mussels and urchins lay strewn in accidental patterns, and out of one such, a nettle grew, a sharp reminder that on this ledge where a life began, it was perhaps the very enormity of the odds against it that spurred one willing survivor to leave the nest at all, to meet the even more challenging world beyond.

Ospreys nesting just a few feet from high tide and looking directly out to sea.

A little farther on, on the East Boothbay side now, we come up on Farnham Point, inside of which is a long cove. Halfway in, there is a wharf with a building on it and beside it, a tall picket fence atop a dam to hold back the water at low tide. This is a lobster pound, an impoundment in which live lobsters are kept by the thousands during periods of low market demand. It is the only such enclosure on the Damariscotta River and was first built by Alan Brown in 1948. I know something about the place because, after a number of years of its disuse, I was hired in 1977 to help rebuild and manage the pound when it was owned by a new company called Ocean Point Lobster.

The depth of water right behind the dam was about six feet at low tide. As the tide rose over the dam, fresh sea water spilled through the pickets and thus refreshed the impounded water twice each day. At one time, we had 42,000 pounds of lobsters in there, which of course represented a whole lot of money, on the hoof so to speak, and as one might imagine, the greater part of my job was to keep those lobsters alive and kicking. I made many a truck run to Stinson Canning in Rockland to pick up loads of herring pieces from the sardine plant. I then salted them in barrels back at the pound. When feeding time came, I rolled a barrel to the edge of the wharf and dumped the whole thing over the side into a very smelly, slippery and disgusting old "pound skiff," which I then rowed round and round, broadcasting the lobster feed as I went.

This particular pound had been known to have poaching problems in the past, which required reconnaissance visits after dark with a spotlight. And the culprits were of various stripes. Some might have worn hats, but I never caught any of them. The primary offenders were raccoons, who patrolled the shallows in the upper end of the cove – their tracks were everywhere. Birds, mostly gulls, were a concern too, of course.

For a period of months, I made regular trips by boat across to the fishermen's co-op in South Bristol, the source of most of our lobsters. Crateful after crateful went into that pound, and as the number of lobsters crept higher and higher, so did the murkiness of the water; 20 or 30,000 lobsters crawling around on muddy bottom can really stir things up. And it becomes harder and harder to see how your investment if faring. Worrisome things work on the pound keeper's mind: Are they getting enough feed? Have they gone "cannibal" on me? Too much feed? Is there a lot of dead fish just rotting down there? What about all those raccoon tracks? How about the salinity with all the fall rains? This cove doesn't have the best circulation in the world. Anything over 10% "shrinkage" (losses) could be disaster.

The time came to have a look, to see what was going on. One brisk December afternoon, I put

The Parade of Boats

Everyone loves a parade, they say, but then it isn't always so. I watch this same parade each autumn and come to the same conclusion each time, that the long, stretched-out procession of boats making its way upriver these several weeks is a sad and reluctant affair.

They're headed up to the boatyard of course, to be hauled out and cradled and made ready for winter … to hibernate through wind and cold and enveloping snow, frozen hard and still, swinging on their moorings no more for the next six or seven months. There's no celebration to this parade. It's more a melancholy line of stragglers who have the appearance, each one as it passes my stretch of shore, of having put off this last up-stream passage until the last possible moment, ever hopeful of having just one more good day on the water.

Most are sailing boats, yawls and ketches and sloops, a schooner or two and some double-ended rigs. Pleasure boats, you might say, and I'd agree, but more importantly, these passing vessels are their owners' favorite possessions, their means of escape from stress and squalor, their best hope of ever being the way we'd all like to be, carefree.

Today I saw three more making their way against a strong north wind, no sails up, just motoring, grimfaced, through the sturdy green waves and a riverful of whitecaps. The sky was leaden between rainsqualls and shafts of sunlight. The backdrop of the far shore was dark green with an overlay of tawny oaks and the pale yellow of birch and paler-still poplars. The entire scene was eerie, beautiful, with a hint of brightness on the horizon, but wild and woolly on the river, where the weather stormed and churned the tide … and did things that would make an artist shrink from trying. It was cold too — raw, numbing.

A clam digger's aluminum skiff whined its way home in the late afternoon, pounding hard and throwing white spray. And then the last boat of the day, one of the parade, ghosted through the trees framing my view – a pale grey ketch with white deckhouse and bare masts. Its little engine droned its last sad song of the season, its bow cutting through those romping, green waves and pushing against the strong wind out of the north, headed upriver for the winter. Sad, yes, but such a wonderful sight. Silently, I cheered.

Friendship Sloop hustling upriver to spend the winter.

on my diving gear and jumped in. The good news was: I found what I had hoped to find – plenty of healthy looking lobsters. The bad news – if one should call it that – was that the visibility on the bottom of the pound was only two or three feet, at best. And I can vouch for the fact that to descend alone into the murky depths of that cove and suddenly be confronted, at extremely close range, by what my eyes and mind told me were 30,000 lobsters, all grabbing for my most personal body parts … well, let's just say, it was pretty much the spookiest place I've ever been.

Twice now, during our tour, I've made reference to the huge winter storm in February, 1978. Well, it was that same year. When I got to the pound at the height of that storm, having made my way through deep, heavy snow, I was met with the alarming sight of a solid half-acre of ice sloshing up and down the length of the cove as though it were in a giant bathtub. It was high tide, exceptionally high, and the incoming wave surges were tremendous. The dam and picket fence had very little dampening effect; the result was that the ice, with each retreating wave, kept smashing against that fence (made of rough-sawn 2x3s) with the altogether expected outcome of splintering it at every blow. There wasn't much that could be done except watch and wait and hope. The tide dropped. The storm abated. The fence held. We were lucky.

Fog on a sunny day. From the Gut looking toward Linekin Neck

89

Window on the Dawn

Every morning as I brush my teeth, I stand looking out the window over my sink at the river, just a stone's throw across the lawn. It's not a passive scene – soothing to my dishevelment at that hour, yes – but rather an active scene of the running tide, the new dawn's weather and creatures beginning their day.

A nosy relative once opened my medicine cabinet and exclaimed in a suspicious tone, "What on earth've you got binoculars in the bathroom for?"

I waved my hand toward the window. "To look at stuff," I told him.

"Yeah, sure," he said, giving me the once-over. "You weirdo!"

My cousin didn't understand a lot of things, such as why I had a window over my sink in the first place, instead of a mirror, and why the weather radio and the tide calendar on the window sill, and the thermometer just outside, up under the eaves. For him, bathrooms are for splashing water and for fooling around with his armpits.

No, he didn't understand at all, and if he could see me standing there in the gloom of dawn, reconnoitering the state of the world at daybreak without turning on any lights, toothbrush hanging out of my mouth, binocs glued to my eyeballs, and stark naked, he'd probably be off alerting the rest of our multitudinous family.

But that's how I begin my days. If the tide is down, there are legions of gulls and herons out there, working the mudflats, crows making their raucous fuss over whatever bothers them the most. It's a whole congregation of purposeful fishers whose devotion to feeding builds with the growing light. If the tide is up, the activity of the shorebirds is curtailed and replaced by the surge of sea water that swells to fill the river valley, daily reinforcing the awareness of ebb and flow I seem unable to escape.

In winter, old squaws, eiders, whistlers, and buffleheads work the patches of open water where the ice has yielded to the current. The sight of them diving among the drifting ice cakes is, as my wife puts it, "like watching National Geographic every morning."

There is one inert element out there – a large rock, or rather, a boulder. It is about eight feet tall and shaped like an egg, standing by itself in the mudflat with its pointed end uppermost. Ordinarily, such a boulder would not attract much attention, but this one is a very prominent feature on our waterfront. In summer, we swim out to stand on it and play King of the Rock. And various friends, arriving by boat at high tide, peer worriedly about them and shout, "Where the hell did that rock go?" Its immovable nature has not gone unnoticed.

By the time January and February roll around, our part of the Damariscotta is pretty well frozen over. Locked to the shore, the expanse of ice does not move, except up and down with the tide. And that is when the big boulder is in its glory, twice a day punching a large hole in the ice, no matter how thick, making its presence known and maintaining a spot of open, lagoon green water.

Kind of mundane stuff for my cousin and the others who can't relate to such things, who haven't windows over their bathroom sinks, who think that early morning hour of the day is for primping and pruning vanity. They could be right … or it could be the mere difference between a mirror and a window; you see what you see.

Artist's scene in the eastern Gut

A far cry from that is the hubbub of our final stop in East Boothbay, the most built-up and industrialized settlement on the Damariscotta River. Thus far we have cruised through a true fishing harbor in the South Bristol Gut, taken a gander at the yachts in Christmas Cove, and now, to cap my tour, I like to give my companions a chance to stare at the big boats bulging through the shop doors of East Boothbay's famous shipyards. The ship-building tradition of this place goes back at least 200 years, and, in that time, probably 600 or more vessels of all types have been launched here.

One of the old yards was Goudy and Stevens, whose history spanned from the age of sail to the modern ships of today. Many a sailing schooner and fishing boat came to life on their site; yawls and cutters too; and motor launches like the 26 foot *Olive*. During the second world war, they built a 165 foot wooden minesweeper, and in 1967, a replica of the near mythical yacht, *America*. The yard finally closed its doors a dozen years ago, but even in the end, it was turning out some interesting work. One such was the 123 foot oil skimmer, *Valdez Star*. Destined for Alaska, it was the largest of its kind ever built. Their very last vessel, *Reliance,* with an elevated pilot house and drop-down bow, was designed to land heavy equipment and vehicles on remote Maine islands. The Goudy and Stevens property was acquired by Hodgdon Brothers Shipyard in 1999.

Hodgdon Yachts, as it is known today, is recognized worldwide for the quality of its productions. It, too, is a very old yard with a long and illustrious story to tell. One of the more famous vessels to come down its ways, in 1921, was the historic exploration schooner, *Bowdoin*, which made 26 arctic voyages under the auspices of the Carnegie Institution, National Geographic and the U.S. Navy, and is still sailing today.

Much more recently, two spectacular yachts have been launched there in just the last few years, coming out of the yard's brand new, state-of-the-art facility. Heightening anticipation among the locals, the big boat shop doors are often wide open, giving riff-raff like us tantalizing glimpses of the caliber of boat-building that has put East Boothbay on the world map. The first (in 1999) was the 124 foot sloop, *Antonisa*, which I don't hesitate to say is probably the most aesthetically perfect looking boat I ever laid eyes on. Next (in 2003) was *Sheherazade*, a 155 foot ketch, launched in a pea soup fog so thick most of us milling around in our boats never saw it happen. Gorgeous as she was though, once the fog lifted, I decided she had been even more pleasing to the eye out of water where the lines of her hull could be fully appreciated.

The Schooner Bowdoin ghosting along in a light wind

93

Next door to Hodgdon Yachts is the patched up old building that used to house Rice Brothers Shipyard – another of those "so ugly, it's beautiful" structures. It is now Washburn and Doughty. Rather than sleek yachts that could be said to require care and upkeep standards approaching obsessive-compulsiveness, Washburn and Doughty builds ferry boats, tugs, fishing and research vessels, which, almost by definition, are designed to take a beating – big, rugged, utilitarian and all steel. As of this writing, 18 of their last 20 hulls were tugs – no yard on the east coast, possibly the whole U.S., builds more – and nothing takes much more of a beating than a tugboat. Two 92 footers caught my eye not so long ago. One was *James R. Moran*, designed to push tankers around and equipped with a pair of pretty serious looking, fire fighting water cannons. The other was a beauty named *Rainbow*. To sidle up in the shadow of such a vessel in a small boat, gawking at all its ladders and handrails, the size of its fenders, hawse pipes and bollards, its huge exhaust stacks and brand new paint job is … well … damned impressive. It kind of makes me proud to know my home river gives birth to such things.

"Rainbow" and the "Kayee Moran" built at
Washburn & Doughty in East Boothbay

The balance of East Boothbay's waterfront is pretty much used up by the Ocean Point Marina's slips and fuel dock, across from the shipyards, and the mooring field in the harbor. Sandwiched between the yards and the marina though is Lobsterman's Wharf restaurant. There was a time when they used to have a good outdoor jazz band there every Sunday during the summer, and waitresses who stepped from boat to boat, taking orders. Despite the tiny docking facilities, it was not unusual to have 15 or 20 boats ganged up, a lot of them friends, to laze away half the afternoon, eating, drinking and visiting, and enjoying the great music. Apparently insurance liability concerns put an end to that ritual, but even still, as I make my way out of the harbor to finally head back upriver for home, I can hear the strains of the *Muskrat Ramble* in my mind.

End of the day at Lobsterman's Wharf, East Boothbay

Two of East Boothbay's finest

It is about now that I usually goose the throttle. Having spent the last four hours thrilling at all the sights while enduring my rambling narrative, my crew, it appears to me, is in need of a pick-me-up. So I treat them to a fast trip straight up the middle of the river just like "Wild Bill." That seems to have the desired effect. The new pace kind of jiggles the mood on board, and there's a round of enthusiastic gushing about all we've seen and done today.

Slowly, though, I notice a change in us all. Usually by the end of the afternoon, the breeze has died down, and the surface of the river goes flat. The heightened tone of the engine at speed, coupled with the swish of water spraying in our wake as we skim over the glassy surface, encloses us in the cocoon of our own sound. My passengers fall silent, just looking and thinking to themselves, perhaps a bit tired after their day on the water. I turn my head to see if Susan is asleep with her book yet. She is.

Whistler

As the late fall afternoon wore on, it grew chilly and still, and the river settled into its evening mood. As often happens at that time of day, I looked up from what I was doing to see what the sky had to offer in the way of a sunset over the hills on the far shore. And what I saw was utter perfection – a clear, uncluttered horizon of continuous, unbroken silhouettes of dark pines and oaks on the ridges, backlit by the purest salmon red sky, with not a wisp of cloud anywhere. The sun was almost gone.

I quit my post in the woodshed doorway and went out to the point to watch, acting on my firm belief that I cannot fully experience a sunset from afar, or from indoors. I must get as close to it as possible. I must be there, to smell the smells, to feel the chill as it settles with the horizon's shadow, to hear the stillness and to see, with all clarity, every ray of light and every reflection suspended on the evening tide.

I sat on some dry grass and leaned back against the trunk of a large pine whose roots grappled with the bank. The last of the sun's highlights fell on the little island just to the north. Rich, deep russets and ambers glowed – autumn's sweet sorrow – and the tall, dead snag stood weathering against the green of December's pines, etched here and there by the white lines of birches.

The sky grew darker and the red afterglow richer. Every shape, the reflection of the trees and the sky on the water, even the occasional barking of the dog across the river, came to me with a crisp clarity so sharp that I was swallowed whole in the mood of this place, and the moment. I was part of it.

The river then turned glassy and black, the only movement its gently swirling eddies, as long lines of gulls began to labor downriver to wherever they spend the chilly nights. Their departure signaled the last moments of the day. Still I sat – something so magnificent as this sunset must take its gradual leave. Even to slowly stand up seemed too abrupt. I just watched and listened.

Only the thinnest sliver of red now remained over the tree line. A few stars brightened. I thought of getting up. And then … *sweswesweswesweswes weswesweswe* … barely audible at first … *sweswesweswesweswesweswe* … growing to become a clean ribbon of sound, a lone whistler duck winged downriver, beating heart and muscle, chasing the fleeing light … *sweswesweswesweswesweswe* … it never faltered … just trailed onward and whispered into the night.

Other than the graceful, swooping turns I must steer in order to avoid occasional mats of seaweed and floating logs, our course is pretty much as I said, straight up the middle of the river. That intimacy of the shore close at hand, of being able to hear the cry of the osprey hovering over its nest, of sensing the nervous shifting of wary seals on their ledge, of sharing it all in whispered conversation … is lost. Lost, too, is the time needed to watch unfolding scenes as they happen, to witness their outcome: a gull wrestling with a crab on a rock, two cormorants fighting over a flounder too big for either of them to swallow, a father and his little girl trying to ready their tiny boat for an evening sail, a stretch of thrashing water and a lone angler trying to catch supper. Instead, we speed onward, ever onward, soon to be only a distant whine and the waves of our wake lapping at the shore we left behind.

Ram Island Light

Old iron ladder on Ram Island

It's not at all an unpleasant sensation to run the river, skimming its calm surface. In fact, in the late evening or very early morning, alone, it awakens an ethereal dimension that cannot be experienced in any other way. I maintain, however, there are too many dimensions to this place I call home to squander them too often in a thirty-minute, twelve-mile dash. Too many. It has not escaped my notice that those who live on and work the Damariscotta for all it's worth, including people, are seldom in a hurry. There is an air of preoccupation. They are immersed in this world of theirs, paying close attention to everything around them. For most creatures, it's simply a matter of survival and seizing the moments of contentment allotted to their existence. For the rest of us, it's having the good fortune to recognize a miracle that can never be taken for granted.

At the end of so many of my days, I put the boat on the mooring, and, as I row ashore in the dinghy, find myself just leaning on the oars, listening to the quiet and looking at the sunset. And then I trudge up to the house and go in. After a few moments and some words to Susan and perhaps getting myself something to drink, I go back out to sit on the kitchen stoop … and watch the river in the twilight, until it disappears.

Flight in a Storm

At the height of an ocean storm, I stood on a point of land that reached far out into the wintry sea. Broad, heaving mountains of beryl green thundered down on the naked ledges with a power that promised to one day devour the bedrock itself. Even in retreat, their seething foam hissed in the violent wash. The tremendous pounding and the trembling ground under my feet riveted me in place as I tried to comprehend the force and energy of the tempest that wielded this power as far as the horizon and beyond.

I tried to imagine, too, the nightmare of waving kelp and rolling boulders down below in the boil of bubbles and sand, as urchins and mussels were ripped from their ground, to be crushed to bits by drift logs in this tireless assault on the shore.

Fisherman's Island

The witness, drawn to this spectacle, can only wonder what it might mean to flounder in those waves and to ride their surge to what end. Even as he ponders such intimacy, he is beckoned forward by the sting of salt spray borne on the wind, and his eye is transported to the colossus of them all, a black giant that grows into a yawning, foam-spewing mountain.

I saw this wave and watched it grow, far offshore. It was moving fast, and before it, a deep valley spread along its white-streaked flanks until it attained near holy proportions. Its vast, glassy slope mounted to a monstrous, curling height, and the raging gale tore at its top ridge, flinging spume far out ahead in long streamers.

And then this terrifying beauty gathered itself ever higher into an awesome wall of pale green, and as it hung poised over my point of land, the moment lingered, and downwind from the north and east came a long white and brown line of eiders, weaving to the powerful thrumbeat of their wings. Twenty or thirty of them, headed somewhere important in the storm, had set on their course down the coast, and, unmindful of the heaving seas only inches below their throbbing breasts, they threaded valleys and skimmed the watery peaks to arrive precisely at the moment the yawning chasm was opened before me.

Down into it they flew, and the glistening dark secrets of the bottom of the sea churned briefly in view as the waters leaped high into the curling wave. With determined wingbeats, the eiders hurtled through, and the gigantic wall of green ocean roared and fell over them in a long, silvery curtain that tore down its length in a thundering flash.

And the eiders beat on. Out the far end they emerged, unimpeded. Like the knotted tail of a kite, they veered gracefully over the boiling turmoil under their wingtips, and in another moment they were gone, disappeared in the trough of yet another sea farther on.

The giant wave spent itself on the granite faces in booming explosions of drenching spray that blew off into the spruces behind me, and all that remained slid back into the sea in rivers and torrents and was swallowed by the storm.

Fisherman's Island

Islands

There is a place in my consciousness separate from the rest of reality; it's an island in my mind. And it is a real island. For a stretch of summers beginning in 1959, I was the hired boy on Cow Island over in Muscongus Bay. I cut trails, painted boats, mowed grass, fished for mackerel, went lobstering, dug clams, rode to the mainland for gas and groceries, and in my free time (which was plentiful), I became so intimately familiar with every inch of the island's shore and woods and the waters around it that my connection with the place bordered on the spiritual. I spent long hours on my own and never wanted for a moment to be anywhere else. The memories and feelings will never leave me, as those were some of the happiest days of my life. Just a glimpse of spruce covered islands gives me pangs of longing to return to that life and to the freedom I had while I was there.

Visually, they are pure miracles, the way they just pop up and sit on the surface, sometimes levitating above it on a shimmering mirage. It seems islands have an aura we are unable to turn our backs on. Despite the inconveniences and logistical difficulties involved with island living, it is quite apparent that they are more than worth the trouble. Perhaps half of our islands are lived on at least a portion of the year, while virtually all the rest are visited regularly. There is no question, their natural beauty and the romantic existence they offer (even for short visits) add immeasurably to the unique character of the Maine coast, its bays and rivers.

On the Damariscotta, its islands are like punctuation marks. They are the common reference points on every passage from beginning to end. There are ten islands of any size within the river proper, four with houses occupied during the summer months, plus quite a number of rocky nubbles supporting grass and perhaps a few trees. I know that most, if not all, are regularly visited by picnickers and occasional campers, who possibly have a favorite spot, as we do, where the anchorage is good, the swimming excellent and where there just happens to be a wide and very thin slab of rock stashed in the bushes to be used as a griddle over the fire.

Beyond the confines of the main river (where the shores lie on both sides), yet bathed in its waters, are still ten more outer islands. And because I consider the areas east of The Gut in South Bristol and around Rutherford Island very much a part of the Damariscotta River environs, I take the liberty here to add an additional half dozen. Thus the Damariscotta encompasses a total of about twenty-six islands and a broad

The Outer Islands seen from the mouth of Little River

The lifesaving station at Damariscove Island

assortment of nubbles. Of the outer islands that stand out to sea, several are lived on a good part of the year, and of those, some are home to whole communities.

Perhaps best known of the Damariscotta River islands is Damariscove, our largest and outermost island. It has the longest and most colorful (if confused) history, including ghosts, going back to the first known European encampment in 1614. And that may well be a big part of the enchantment it holds for all of us who land there. The island's resources were abundant enough to support farm settlements, and the fishing was excellent. A very important factor in its being chosen for a foothold in this "new" world was its distance from the mainland, which was of some comfort against the threat of attack by the not-always-friendly natives.

The Museum at Damariscove Island

Today, Damariscove has very much the atmosphere of a preserve with marked hiking trails, instructive signs and even a tiny museum. On approaching the island, there is a sense of power in its bold aspect and, for me, the inescapable feeling that dramatic events have taken place on this rocky outpost. My most intimate and exhilarating experience out there was on a summer excursion with a group from the National Marine Fisheries Service, who were monitoring an experiment using old tires as artificial "burrows" for lobsters. We dove off the east side of the island in about ninety feet of water. The tires were indeed fulfilling their new role in life, as there were a number of lobsters in them.

But what I best remember was the jumbled, rocky slope of the island bounding down, down to the bottom of pure sand. It was surprisingly bright, and the visibility must have been 50 or 60 feet. There were lavender horse mussels, starfish, sea urchins, anemones, algae of all descriptions and an old bottle encrusted with gigantic barnacles. I think what most impressed me, though, were the

truly huge ripples on that sandy bottom. They were perhaps two feet high. That was powerful evidence of the force of the pounding North Atlantic, its waves roiling that island's flanks and stirring the sand at that depth to build it into such magnificent windrows.

For such a large island, it has only one narrow, protected harbor at the extreme southern tip, which, from a small boat, can seem to be at the edge of the world. The old Coast Guard lifesaving station there, dating back to 1897, has been newly restored to a state of respectability, though it no longer functions in its former capacity. Looking out to sea through the haze toward Monhegan and beyond, there is nothing but the Atlantic. Somewhere in the remote distance and the remote past, is the old world where our ancestors voyaged out from to find this place. That was four hundred years ago. There is a feeling about Damariscove, its ghosts, its name, the centuries it has witnessed, standing emblematic sentry at the mouth of this river I live on.

Acknowledgements

It goes without saying, much of what I know and feel about the Damariscotta River has to do with the company I keep and those with whom I have shared a deep appreciation of it. A complete list of those people would be very lengthy indeed. To the following, however, I am indebted for their direct involvement in this project.

For their colorful descriptions and insight into historical matters, I especially want to thank Bruce Farrin; Paul Bryant; Ronald House; Jack French; Penny Walker; Katherine and Chester Rice; my old buddies from the Darling Center, Gil Jaeger and Warren Riess; and Barbara Seefeld, who first arrived on this river the old-fashioned way, by ship.

For their very willing assistance in helping me to fill in certain blanks in my knowledge, I am grateful to Cecil Burnham; Mary Trescot; John Mitchell; Bruce Farrin Jr.; Rebecca Brown; and John Wood, who apparently yells a lot and fed me the nice detail of the echo at Carlisle Island.

I thank Robert Reed for official permission to trespass on the property of Anne and Peter Weller; and, for the same courtesy, Gretchen Hartzog, who once during a telephone conversation, held her phone out the window for me to hear the storm waves on the Thread of Life.

To my excellent friend Mike Rosenthal, who rivals me in his appreciation of fine sunsets, I owe a huge personal debt for reading every single word of this text and wisely advising me to toss quite a lot of it … and to fix the rest.

My son, Elijah – little did he realize when he wrote an essay for school, years ago, about the river and how it had been the common thread coursing through his life as we moved from place to place – gave me the first inspiration for this effort.

Then there's Susan, my dear wife, who has seen it all by my side. Thanks, Hon, for everything.

The Damariscotta River Buoy at the mouth of Little River with Washburn & Doughty's tug "Little Toot" out for a toot.

Photographer's Statement

One rainy afternoon in October of 2003, I took a short cruise on the upper Damariscotta River with Barnaby Porter and Gus Johnson aboard Gus's trawler, *Shinola*. I had with me a newly acquired digital camera.

The very next day, Barnaby and I boarded his boat, *Old Crow*, for an extended trip downriver to the Gamage Shipyard for fuel. Cruising at Barnaby's normal speed, coined "coving" by a hard-driving friend, we took our sweet time getting there and back. Again, I had the camera.

Later in my studio, I was quite pleased to find several keepers among the two hundred or so images I'd shot. Some of those are included in this book. Many trips and two cameras later, we started to talk about what we should do with this growing library of photographs. A show? A book? Maybe both. We let it hibernate over the winter.

In the spring of 2004, we set out with more purpose. Our photo-shoots started early and ended past sunset. I came back with five or six hundred images per trip and kept records of where we'd been and what we saw. All the while, Barnaby narrated stories and impressions that went with those images, things that only someone having his relationship with the river would know.

The Damariscotta River is only just over the hill from where I live. Finally getting to know it and creating this book has been a rich and rewarding experience. When we began this project, it seemed it would be mostly photographs, and I wondered if they would be enough. Pushing Barnaby to write something, I was pleased to see that his words and my pictures complimented each other. The Damariscotta River really created this book. Barnaby's and my roles were to put it to paper.

I want to thank my wife, Mary, for her constant enthusiasm and encouragement. A couple of weeks ago, I told her I was beginning to tire of some of my photographs. She said it was time to publish them. Here they are. She was right.

Al Trescot
Damariscotta Maine
March 21, 2005

Colophon: *Twelve Miles* is set in Adobe Brioso Pro. Captions are in Gil sans light italic. Page layout with Adobe InDesign CS. Imaging with Adobe Photoshop CS. Stochastic printing by J.S. McCarthy of Augusta, Maine, USA.